Wealth of Self and Wealth of Nations

Wealth of Self and Wealth of Nations:
Self-Axis of the Great Ascent

SECOND EDITION

Philip McShane

M.Sc., Lic. Phil., S.T.L., D. Phil. Oxon.

edited by
James Duffy

AXIAL PUBLISHING
Vancouver

Axial Publishing
2-675 Victoria Drive
Vancouver, British Columbia
V5L 4E3 Canada
www.axialpublishing.com

Canadian Cataloguing in Publication Data
McShane, Philip, 1932–2020
Wealth of Self and Wealth of Nations

ISBN   978-1-988457-09-3
1. Methodology   2. Philosophy   I. Title

Text layout and cover:
James Gerard Duffy

To Bernard Lonergan,
in his seventieth year,
and
for Fiona

"Marx was wrong in his diagnosis of the manner in which capitalist society would break down; he was not wrong in the prediction that it would break down eventually."

Joseph A. Schumpeter
Capitalism, Socialism, & Democracy
Third Edition, Harper, New York, 1950
pp. 424–5

Table of Contents

Diagrams and Heuristics

Editor's Introduction

The first edition of *Wealth of Self and Wealth of Nations* was published in 1975,[1] a few years after two other works by McShane on empirical methodology—*Randomness, Statistics, and Emergence*[2] and *Plants and Pianos*.[3] While there are a handful of references to those two prior works scattered throughout the current book, it was not written for Oxford professors or for a conference gathering of professional philosophers and theologians; nor was it written to initiate dialogue between schools of philosophy. *WSWN* is an introductory book[4] and the author's primary aim is to "dialogue with you about you."[5]

There is, however, at least one important similarity among these three books. Like the two previous books, *WSWN* could have been subtitled "Towards an Adequate *Weltanschauung*."[6] A decent view from the peak of Everest or Denali (formerly Mt. McKinley) is had only after much training and a long, slow, and possibly perilous ascent—it takes about two months to get a peak view from Everest, about three weeks to get one from Denali. *WSWN* is something of a climber's guide for those willing to ascend. As indicated by the subtitle, the axis of the ascent is you.

In chapter 1, McShane considers the existence of personal horizons and appeals for an acknowledgement of a new horizon. He then proceeds to invite you to "climb" by appropriating the dynamics of what-ing (chapters 2 and 3), is-ing (chapters 4 and 5), what-to-do-ing (chapter 6), believing (chapter 7), conveniently symbolizing (chapter 8), and imaginatively exploring potentialities for a larger human life (chapter 9). Underpinning reflection and personal appropriation throughout, and finally made explicit, is the notion of survival (chapter 10).

Besides reading the various topics treated throughout the text and attempting the various exercises, you are invited to "read" yourself. "So, for example, not merely are you invited to laboriously discover the rule behind a technique for getting square roots: more pertinently you are invited to a detailed discovery of yourself in the phases of that discovery."[7] To aid the double reading, there are diagrams and equations scattered throughout the text. There are also references to any number of philosophers, economists, poets, novelists, and literary critics, and intimations of ways they contribute to the appropriation of precious personal assets. Such references are to encourage the adventure. For example, McShane cites Aquinas regarding the way we humans try to understand the simplest or most complex data—by forming "phantasms" or images—and cites Heidegger regarding a forgetfulness of being, which is at once nearest to humans and yet remains farthest removed.[8] These and other citations are part of an invitation to 'taste and see.' Obviously no author or teacher can do that for you. All they can do is invite, "present the sensible elements in the issue in a suggestive order and with a proper distribution of emphasis,"[9] and pose questions, e.g., **why** does the environment "out there" seem to jump around when I close one eye, place a finger on lower ridge of the eye socket of the other eye, and gently move my eyeball up and down?[10]

The process of mining self-assets can be likened to the process of slowly, sometimes painfully gaining a bit of clarity in a heart-to-heart with a friend or with a therapist—assuming the friend or therapist has courageously[11] done some self-searching clarification herself or himself.[12] Being gentle with my 'nearest neighbor' is by no means a cake walk. I have been "talked into talk by those who talk at me" and will never "unweave the web to the very bottom."[13] Not all of the talk has been kind or truthful, so, yes, it takes faith and courage to discover that "I have a universe inside me / Where I can go and spirit guide me / Then I can ask oh any question."[14] Embracing little humdrum exercises in twofold attention provides a glimpse of intentional existence of a second phase of the temporal subject when "one is by one's own intention the subject of one's intellectual nature both as actuated and as to be actuated further."[15]

In chapter 10 McShane claims that a change of framework, or point of view, is both possible and desirable if we humans are to survive. In the Epilogue he notes that a viewpoint "can develop only slowly, and its emergence is at times more genetical, at times more dialectical, depending on one's teacher, temperament, tribulations, and traditions."[16] At the same time, he recognizes a central paradox: whether it is Plato,[17] Joan Robinson,[18] or Robert Heilbroner[19] writing about, possibly imploring a change in point of view, such a change is often difficult to identify. There is an existential dimension to reading a book or listening to a song. I might read but not understand; I might hear but not be in a position to listen very well. Likewise, you and I might visit the Museum of Modern Art together and be drawn out of the space of the workaday world into the space of different paintings—you into Van Gogh's *The Starry Night* and I into Picasso's *Les Demoiselles d'Avignon*.

That a radical change in viewpoint is needed is a remarkable claim. Surely young students can pursue a degree in one or other social science at the London School of Economics or some other prestigious university without meta-

inquiring about the assets of the laughing, inquiring social animal researching social issues and social policies, can't they? Surely the social sciences as currently taught and practiced—without an inkling of "cultural overhead,"[20] time to leisurely appreciate and develop technico-aesthetic and aesthetico-technic personal assets[21]—are not peculiarly dangerous and mad, are they?[22]

In the "second movement" mentioned in the Epilogue, McShane introduces symbolism for studying individuals and human history.[23] He writes that symbolism is part of a "reorientation of one's science, common sense, and the symbolic filling out of a slow-growing-adequate personal *Weltanschauung*." Although the symbolism might appear strange at first, it protects those studying organisms against both reductionism and Platonic vitalism.[24]

Diagrams also play a role in our climb towards an adequate viewpoint. In chapter 5, "The Inside-Out of Radical Existentialism," McShane provides a diagram that "represents you, the organism."[25] Years later he named the middle box of this diagram "mibox."[26] In *Interpretation from A to Z*, he identified the challenge of reading the diagram slowly, very slowly, and recalled his answer to his 44-month-old grandson Matthew who asked Grandpa what his superpower was:

> My superpower is walking slowly. My superpower is definitely best illustrated by my personal walking slowly in and round and about versions of that diagram for half a century, and still in a state of W. W? Walking in and into slowly, Wondering slowly, Wanting slowly, Wising-up slowly, Willing so.[27]

James Duffy

Notes

[1] Hicksville, NY: Exposition Press. [Hereafter *WSWN*.]

[2] *Randomness, Statistics, and Emergence*, the original manuscript of McShane's D.Phil. thesis, was first published in 1970 by Macmillan and University of Notre Dame Presses. A second edition, edited by James Duffy and Terrance Quinn, was published in 2021 by Axial Publishing. [References in the editor's introduction are to the second edition, hereafter *RSE*.] *RSE* was written in Oxford "and draws on

that background" (*RSE*, lxiii) to initiate a dialogue between different schools of philosophy, to reorient philosophy of science "from within" (ibid.), to elucidate and supplement the principle of "emergent probability" (CWL 3, 144–151), and finally "to establish on a wider basis of contemporary mathematics and science the position of B. Lonergan on the nature of randomness, statistics, and emergence." *RSE*, lxiv.

3 *Plants and Pianos: Two Essays in Advanced Methodology*, Dublin, Milltown Institute, 1971, was written prior to The First International Lonergan Congress that took place the first week of March, 1970, in Boca Raton, Florida. At that gathering McShane presented "Metamusic and Self-Meaning," the second essay in *Plants and Pianos*, which he had completed the year before in Oxford. It was his first effort to identify fragmentation potential and understand the dynamics of the omnidisciplinary collaborative enterprise that Lonergan had discovered in 1965 and published in "Functional Specialties in Theology," *Gregorianum* 50 (1969): 485–504.

4 McShane wrote a number of introductory books: *Towards Self-Meaning* (with Garrett Barden), Dublin, Gill, 1968; *Music That Is Soundless*, Dublin, Milltown Press, 1968; *Process: Introducing Themselves to the Young (Christian) Minders*, Mount St. Vincent Press, 1990; *Economics for Everyone: Das Jus Kapital*, Commonwealth Press, 1996; *Introducing Critical Thinking* (with Alexandra Drage and John Benton), Nova Scotia, Axial Publishing, 2005; *Futurology Express*, Vancouver, Axial Publishing, 2013.

5 Page xi below.

6 "The book [*RSE*] might well have been subtitled *Towards an Adequate Weltanschauung*." *RSE*, lxiv. "Image and Emergence: Towards and Adequate *Weltanschauung*" is the title of chapter 2 of *Plants and Pianos*. McShane likely settled on the subtitle "Self-Axis of the Great Ascent" because of references to Robert Heilbroner's *The Great Ascent: The Struggle for Economic Development in Our Time*.

7 Page 1 below.

8 See pages 82, 88, and 95 below.

9 CWL 3, 29.

10 See pages 35–38 below.

11 "Why should we honour those that die upon the field of battle? A man [or woman] may show as reckless a courage in entering into the abyss of himself [or herself]." William Butler Yeats.

12 See endnotes 9 and 10 in the Introduction, below on page xiii below.

13 Austin Farrer, *Love Almighty and Ills Unlimited*, London, Collins, 1967, 114.

14 Sinead O'Connor, "The Healing Room," from the album *Faith and Courage*.

15 CWL 12, 405, symbolized by "DDT XII Q. 21." The text is cited in endnote 15 of chapter 1 on page 7 below.

[16] Epilogue, page 92 below. N.B.: The word "genetic" is here used in the classic sense of *genesis* or development rather than to the more recent meaning relating to genes.

[17] The *periagogue* that Socrates speaks of in the *Republic* (518c-d, 530c, 532b) has been translated "turn around," "reversal," or "conversion." I prefer either of the first two translations to the loaded third. The word "displacement" is also a possibility.

[18] "It is time to go back to the beginning and start again." Joan Robinson and John Eatwell, *An Introduction to Modern Economics*, London and New York, McGraw Hill, 1973, 52.

[19] "We must lift ourselves out of our accustomed American frame of reference and catapult ourselves across a distance wider than the oceans that separate us from the continents in which the struggle for development is taking place." *The Great Ascent*, New York, Harper & Row, 148, cited at the beginning of chapter 10, page 77 below.

[20] The phrases "overhead profit" and "cultural overhead" are typically not used by economists such as Jeffrey Sachs, Amartya Sen, Joseph Stiglitz, Paul Krugman, Thomas Piketty, and Francis Fukuyama; and you will not find the phrases in the textbooks of Gregory Mankiw and Thomas Sowell or in the popular books of Milton Friedman and Alan Greenspan. In order to distinguish "the ordinary final product of standard of living" from "the overhead final product of cultural implements" (Bernard Lonergan, *For a New Political Economy*, vol. 21, Collected Works of Bernard Lonergan, ed. Philip McShane, Toronto: University of Toronto Press, 1998, 20), one needs to clearheadedly distinguish basic and non-basic goods and services as well as basic and non-basic stages of the productive process, and identify different economics phrases. The basic insights leading to a normative meaning of "new leisure" (ibid., 19) are accessible to high school students. See the next note.

[21] These are the titles of chapter 8 and 9 respectively. In chapter 7 McShane focuses on the economy of truth, or belief. An invitation to appropriate the basic insights of sane economics is found in McShane's later writings. See, for example, Chapter One: The Key Elementary Class, *Sane Economics and Fusionism*, Vancouver, Axial Publishing, 2010, 17–25; Chapter 1 "The Key Issue," *Piketty's Plight and the Global Future*," Vancouver, Axial Publishing, 2014, 5–14; and the "Preface to the 2017 Edition" (3rd ed.) of *Economics for Everyone: Das Jus Kapital*, Vancouver, Axial Publishing, 2017, i–xiii.

[22] I articulated my opposition to the madness in "Minding the Economy of Campo Real," *Divyadaan: Journal of Philosophy & Education*," vol. 29, no. 1, 2018, 1–24.

[23] See pages 91–91 below.

[24] McShane later replaced the commas in the diagrams of humans and history that appear in the Epilogue with semicolons. See, e.g., *Cantower* XXIX, "Physics and Other Sciences," where he identifies the "huge task of the specialty Communications to nudge culture towards an understanding and an operative sense of the meaning of ' ; ', a sense that would identify our world as aggreformic, which would expose the nonsense in both reductionism and vitalism" (15). The importance of the symbolism for McShane is reflected in his decision in the spring of 2008 to write forty-one *Field Nocturne* essays to properly read a single paragraph in *Insight* that begins "Study of the organism begins from the thing-for-us, from the organism as exhibited to our senses." CWL 3, 489.

[25] See page 36 below.

[26] "Let us not get heavily into identifying, self-identifying, the mibox for the moment. Suffice it to note, at whatever level you can, that the mibox is the middle box of the inside box. It is the WHAT box, with wonder driving up through the molecules to it and beyond. It is the what that, in its fullness, asks, "What might be?" *Interpretation* 10: "The Genetics of Genetics in Mibox" (available at http://www.philipmcshane.org/interpretation), 2.

[27] *Interpretation from A to Z*, 142–143.

Preface

"Sufficient for the day is the newspaper thereof"[1] is cuttingly close to a particular trend toward the confinement of mind in modern times. In daily overdose the popular press selects events significant to the marketing of its established ideology and itself. There need be no malice, even if the ideology be as extreme as that of Peking: but, self-justification, even though implicit, certainly. Moreover, "the basic form of ideology is the self-justification of alienated man,"[2] and since the normal mode of contemporary man is the mode of alienation, that basic form of ideology is the color of our daily print. Not only indeed of our daily print: Galbraith's *Estate of the Mind*[3] is far from an immune elite.

An immediate comment on the title of this present work will help to place it in relation to this vicious circulation of ideology. The title may be related most obviously to two works by the American economist Robert L. Heilbroner, *The Great Ascent: The Struggle for Economic Development in Our Time*[4] and "The Paradox of Progress: Decline and Decay in *The Wealth of Nations*."[5] In this latter essay on *The Wealth of Nations* Heilbroner brings out the fact that, despite the genius of the book as a charter document in the development of the social sciences, "Smith was hobbled by a class-bound social vision" and was "a product of his time."[6] Meshed, then, with the problem of alienation is the problem of relativism. Both are large problems, yet it is with these that this small book deals. Its thesis, briefly, is that the core of non-alienating self-justification and nonrelative perspective and precepts lies in the adequate heuristic objectification of the self.

Between the statement and reading of this thesis and its appreciation is a long haul. For, its appreciation is equivalent to a non-alienating self-justification, to the adequate objectification of invariants of the self. Here the reader will have noticed, for the first of many times, a peculiar twist to the book. The twist is intimate to the thesis and the title. The axis is the self-axis, our twentieth century is itself axial, and future dimensions of human well-being depend on present quarrying in that wealth of self.

But questions of invariance and the like belong more to the conclusion of an introductory book than to its preface. One point I would, however, emphasize both here and in the conclusion: that this work is merely an introduction. It is an introduction to a methodology which can be identified, in my view, with an adequate metaphysics. The introduction has a metaeconomic slant but it is in fact general: there is an invariant core to any particular meta-questioning. So it is that certain sections of the present book parallel previous contributions to an introduction.[7]

This appears clearly from a comparison of chapter headings in the two books: the titles of the first five chapters are almost equivalent, though the contents here bear the mark of wider interest. Chapter 5, for instance, stresses the issue of objectivity in economics. Chapters 6 through 9 here parallel my contribution of chapters 7, 8, 10, 11 to the previous book, though the titles note a new perspective. But my basic philosophy of behavior and belief, of technology and art remains the same. In chapter 10 I give myself freer rein, and still more in the epilogue, in order to point beyond the introduction to further possibilities of self-searching and of social change. But I must add that my introduction does not take sides: my interest is in the questing-structure of the reader whatever his or her allegiance. A recent Marxist claim is that "a distinctive feature of the Marxist approach is intensive preoccupation with the structure of cognitive process; keen attention devoted to the continuous search for 'conditions of obtaining truth' in social investigations."[8] Very well, then: be you a Marxist or not let me ask you for a little keen attention to yourself, and your conditions for obtaining and creating truth.

I had a great idea of bringing this introduction out as a single newspaper—it would in fact be quite a small paper. But then it would take a year and a day to read.[9] So of course would any newspaper if one were rooting after its meaning. I recall once commenting in newsprint on Joyce, "More power to Joyce who has foxed the nations for thirty years with that multiple-single endless-beginningless word called *Finnegans Wake*."[10] I think *The Wake* can teach us something about reading. Perhaps this little book can, too. I can only try, and hope now that I have stirred your curiosity to echo Joyce and say:

> Your bard's highview, avis on valley! I would like to hear you burble to us in strict conclave, purpurando, and without too much italiote interfairance, what you know in petto about our sovereign beingstalk, Tonans Tomazeus. O dite![11]

Notes

[1] James Joyce, *Ulysses*, New York, Random House, 1986, 129.

[2] Bernard Lonergan, *Method in Theology*, London, Darton, Longman and Todd, 1973, 357; *Method in Theology*, Robert M. Doran and John D. Dadosky (eds.), vol. 14, Collected Works of Bernard Lonergan, Toronto, University of Toronto Press, 2017, p. 330.

[3] *The New Industrial State*, Princeton University Press, 1967, chapter XXV.

[4] New York, Harper and Row, 1963.

[5] *Journal of the History of Ideas*, 34 (1973), 243–262.

[6] Ibid., 261.

[7] *Towards Self-Meaning*, with co-author Garrett Barden, Dublin, Gill Macmillan, 1969.

[8] Zygmunt Bauman, "Modern Times, Modern Marxism," in *Marxism and Sociology, Views from Eastern Europe*, edited by Peter Berger, New York, Appleton-Century-Crofts, 1969, 12.

[9] The suggestion is not superficial. More recently I have found that Marcel Proust had anticipated me. We need, in our times, what Roger Poole calls "hieroglyphs" (*Towards Deep Subjectivity*, New York, Harper and Row, 1972, 16), to manifest counter-objectivity. The theologian F. E. Crowe has remarked that the twenty-fifth century will look back on our newspapers as we look back now on fifteenth-century slavery. And there is the poet Patrick Kavanagh, whose hieroglyphic newspaper lasted only six weeks: "It is impossible to read the daily press without being diverted from reality."

[10] In the monthly newspaper of the Gaelic League *Rosc*, February, 1970, from one of a series of twelve articles (November 1969–October 1970) under the title "Philosophy That Is Mindful" making a plea for rich, local, common meaning.

[11] *Finnegans Wake*, 504.

Introduction

A previous effort at introducing this book began from such disparate events of 1773 as the Boston Tea Party, Pugachev's peasant revolt in Russia, and Kant's correspondence with his friend Marcus Herz.[1] It moved on to mesh together the lives of Hume and Smith and to point to the changes in British ways over these past two centuries. What was being hinted at was the need for perspective. But a hint is adequately echoed only if what is called to mind is already in that mind in relevant fashion. To this problem I will presently return.

My primary concern in the book, as will become continually more evident, is not with history but with my reader. In the preface I remarked that it deals with problems of alienation and relativism. More correctly I am, I hope, dealing with the reader, in dialogue with you about you. I am inviting you to begin a difficult and delicate task of self-investigation that excludes basic alienation. In my ten-chapter invitation to that task my appeals to history or authority occupy no central role. I ask you only, in the words of Kant's letter of 1773 to "make many careful observations. Here as elsewhere, theories are often directed more to the relief of the idea than to the mastery of the phenomenon."[2] And the phenomenon is you. No doubt there are those who will assert that the phenomenon to start with is "the given" and the problem of just what is given. I have, I must admit, little sympathy with debates about the given. What is evidently given is the debate, the problem, and, to quote Hume against himself, "methinks we have been not a little inattentive to run over so many different parts of the human mind, and examine so many passions, without taking once into consideration that love of truth, which was the first source of all our enquiries."[3]

To make the first source of all our enquiries in the myriad categories of its achievement the object of a full-blooded empirical science is to be radical in metaphysics in the twentieth century. The movement represents what I call radical existentialism. Charles James Fox, another figure of 1773, called for radical reform, a reform which slowly gathered momentum with the pressure of nineteenth century radicals. The radical reform of metaphysics goes deeper. Its need is less evident than the needs that Fox noted: slavery of minds is less patent than slavery of body.[4] And my interest is in the abolition of that slavery at its roots.

The underlying question of the present book is that which is raised by the quotation from Schumpeter at its beginning, expressing his view on the end of capitalism. That question is not answered here: sufficient for one small introductory book to invite the prior questioning of core alienation. Without digging up the neglected global asset, the asset in selves, the underlying question cannot, indeed, be adequately posed. Nonetheless, the reader should not remain unaware even at this introductory stage of the dimensions of the undertaking. "Explicit metaphysics is the conception, affirmation and implementation of the integral heuristic structure of proportionate being." [5] Proportionate being includes the England of Hume and Smith, Ricardo and Marx, Darwin and Clerk-Maxwell, Gladstone and Disraeli, Marshall and Keynes. It includes that two-hundred-year span of English history which represents an island version of the emergence and decline of capitalism.[6] More subtly it includes the minds of men of genius, their slow-growing understanding and their implemented plans. Moreover, the heuristic structure regards not only history but what is yet to be, and implementation is an intrinsic component in metaphysics.

To glimpse such dimensions of metaphysics may, for the beginner, be somewhat discouraging. But it gives a realism of challenge to my invitation. Again, a felt challenge to implement some policy for reform is widely present in students: that such commitment to reform is intrinsic to metaphysics as properly conceived should encourage them even if the enormity of the project is alarming.

The percentage of the scientific estate of these closing decades of the twentieth century committed to such metaphysics, and the inadequacy of the alternatives of interdisciplinary schemes, these no doubt are aspects of the present thesis. But they are not our immediate concern. My reader, I hope, is sufficiently impressed by the present challenge to adequate self-justification to raise—what is our concern—a personal question regarding radical existentialism. So I add some further comments to aid in the answering of that question.

Authenticity and radical existentialism are not synonymous. Yet it seems to me that if you have some share in the Academic Estate and wish to enter the twenty-first century neither drifting nor bewildered, you should give radical existentialism at least a serious try.[7] But what is one to regard as a serious try? While the question is yours, not mine, my answer could well be a help.

In the pursuit of wisdom my sympathies are altogether more with Husserl than with Hume. One of my favorite quotations of twentieth-century philosophy is from a letter from Husserl to Franz Brentano, written on his birthday in 1904: "How I would like to live on the heights. For this is all my thinking craves for. But shall I ever work my way upwards, if only for a little, so that I can gain something of a free distant view? I am now forty-live years old, and I am still a miserable beginner."[8]

Hume published his *Treatise on Human Nature* at the age of twenty-seven. At the same age, and in my seventh year of mathematical science and philosophy, I had just been startled by the main point I try to put across here in chapter five. Nor do I cease to be startled: as, more recently, by the dimensions of the assets of the self, their relation on the one hand to rhythms of nature and on the other to creeping socialism and multinational corporations. Again, I have no sympathy with the mentality that assumes that a Ph.D. includes an essential world view—the rest of one's thinking life being footnotes. Lest I get further out on an academic limb, I will halt here. The trouble is, as Maslow has pointed out, that there are not enough specimens around of adult growth[9] and, as A. R. Aresteh remarks: "Unless the psychologist has himself experienced the state of quest of final integration in the succession of identities he will hardly acquire an understanding or incentive for doing research on it."[10]

And here let me return to the question of perspective, the question of having history in mind in relevant fashion. One does not reach adult growth by growing old with cherished memories. One does not reach adequate perspective[11] even by ranging through detailed history. Adequate growth and perspective come forth in a person only if he comes to grips with himself with a degree of seriousness that at present finds little acceptance in academic life.

Marcuse remarks, in the introduction to his *Reason and Revolution*, that after the French revolution "the economic process appeared as the foundation of reason."[12] To propose to stand that viewpoint, literally, on its head, and give priority to psychic and intellectual process[13] would seem to be as foolish now as it was to challenge Say's Law fifty years ago. "Whether or not a person accepted Say's Law was, until the thirties, the prime test by which economists were distinguished from crackpots."[14] Do we have to await a deeper depression to bring us to our minds?

Notes

[1] Immanuel Kant. *Philosophical Correspondence*, 1757–99. Edited and translated by Arnulf Zweig, The University of Chicago Press, 1967, 76.

[2] Ibid.

[3] *A Treatise of Human Nature*, Oxford, 1951, 448.

[4] The abolition of the slave trade, one of Fox's ambitions, was achieved in 1807, the year after his death.

[5] B. Lonergan, *Insight: A Study of Human Understanding*, London, Longmans, Green & Co., 1957, p. 391; *Insight: A Study of Human Understanding*, vol. 3, Collected Works of Bernard Lonergan, Frederick Crowe and Robert Doran (eds.), Toronto, University of Toronto Press, 1992, p. 416. Except for occasional remarks, as in the epilogue, I am restricting my considerations to historical reality in its nonreligious dimensions.

[6] Part V of Joseph A. Schumpeter's *Capitalism, Socialism and Democracy*, New York, Harper, 1950, contains his views of declining capitalism. A preface to the third English edition, 1949, printed at the end, comments on English developments at that time.

[7] I have touched on the modes of authenticity whether one succeeds or not in my introduction to B. Lonergan, *Introducing Bernard Lonergan*, London, Darton, Longman and Todd, 1973. That introduction complements the introduction to the present work.

[8] From a letter of Edmund Husserl to Franz Brentano, October 15, 1904, quoted in H. Spiegelberg, *The Phenomenological Movement*, Vol. I, The Hague, 1965, 89.

[9] *Towards a Psychology of Being*, New York, Van Nostrand, 1968, 204.

[10] *Final Integration in the Adult Personality*, Leiden, E. J. Brill, 1965, 18.

[11] What I have in mind is Perspectivism as explained in the context of the eight functional specializations of Bernard Lonergan. See his *Method in Theology*, index under *Perspectivism*.

[12] H. Marcuse, *Reason and Revolution*, London, Routledge and Kegan Paul, 1963, 4.

[13] Christian theologians will recognize larger dimensions of the stress on the intelligible processions within mind.

[14] J. K. Galbraith, *Economics and the Public Purpose*, Boston, Houghton Mifflin Company, 1973, 21. Economists may disagree with Galbraith's policy suggestions, but his diagnosis is surely not altogether wide of the mark. This present book enters the debate at the personal foundational level. It seeks to contribute to "the Emancipation of Belief" *(op. cit.*, pp. 221 ff.) and to a more remote political economy.

Chapter 1 ~ Horizons

We may formulate the same point (concerning innovation) by means of the concept of Horizon. This we define as that range of choice within which a businessman moves freely and within which his decision for a course of action can be described exclusively in terms of profitability and foresight. It differs widely with different types and individuals. But within a stationary or a growing process, we may assume that the management of each firm commands that horizon which enables it to transact its current business and to handle ordinary emergencies. Outside of such processes, however, horizons of different people differ according to the criterion that the horizons of some are and the horizons of others are not confined to the range of possibilities tried out in business practice.[1]

In his two-volume work *Business Cycles* Schumpeter stressed the importance of innovation and the process of dispersal of novelty. Entrepreneurial initiative harnessed inventivity, what was surprising became evident, and its benefits flowed in widening channels through the economy. Thus, steam power transformed the industry and agriculture of nineteenth-century England. Moreover, innovations like the railways gave rise to long cycles of expansion, as compared with the more usual business cycles recognized by Juglar.[2]

My concern in this book is with an expansion of longer cycle.[3] My problem is that the innovation concerns the core of meaning in oneself; the invention is larger but less palpable than a locomotive, and the benefits range not only beyond present business practice but also largely beyond contemporary academic concerns. My problem briefly is the problem of horizons and so I begin there.

But first a brief appeal. I insist that this book is an effort to introduce a new horizon. Reluctantly, then, I keep illustrations and suggestions elementary, though I expect readers may find them exacting. Insofar as the suggestions are not seriously and self-attentively followed, the reader is not with me. So, for example, not merely are you invited to laboriously discover the rule behind a technique for getting square roots: more pertinently you are invited to a detailed discovery of yourself in the phases of that discovery. We are handicapped here, as I said, by contemporary conventions of meaning. So, for example, when lecturing in mathematical physics I had no need for apology, nor had my students any illusions about the labor involved or the endless examples to be struggled with in order to handle with ease, say, a range of problems of central forces in dynamics. In methodology, however, a much more exacting study, apology is the order of the day. I recall here, I hope helpfully, one of my efforts at apology in the context of a discussion of the patient experimental work being done toward understanding animal thirst:

> The philosopher may learn a lesson from this for his own field: if the understanding of animal thirst is a remote goal of the zoological enterprise, the philosopher should hardly consider the understanding of human understanding or human thirst for understanding as some youthful achievement preliminary to doing his own thing.[4]

This, brief appeal is of course a direct appeal for the acknowledgment of a new horizon of method. But it is time to turn to a more general consideration of the existence of horizons and of the problem of accepting and transcending them.

We may begin with the story of the lady who invited the physicist to tea. As the meal drew to a close, the lady remarked that she had always wanted to understand Einstein's Theory of Relativity, and since she now had a real physicist to talk to, perhaps he could explain it to her. "Of course, I don't know any physics and I always hated mathematics," she said, "so you would have to avoid all that terminology and the use of formulae. But I know you are an excellent physicist, and you surely will be able to explain it to me, in my own simple words." The point of the story is clear—the lady has no conception of what understanding Einstein's theory involves. That the physicist spent years studying before he came to have some understanding of it means little to her. Her horizon is the limited horizon of common sense. Her reaction to what lies outside that horizon may be the extreme one which claims that what is outside her horizon just isn't, or the less extreme one that acknowledges a "beyond" but would hope that whatever is of value "beyond" would surely be capable of contraction to within her horizon.

One might represent diagrammatically the various horizons as concentric circles, the horizon of common sense fitting within the horizon of science. Now I ask the reader to draw yet another outside circle to represent the horizon of methodology. As I have hinted, it is more than likely that the reader will find it hard to accept or envisage such a horizon, but I would hope to bring him to intelligently accept and vaguely envisage it. Is that hope vain? Certainly one should not expect too much. After all, if my claim is correct, my efforts here are rather akin to the efforts of the physicist to explain Einstein to the lady. I would be highly pleased, of course, if you were halted by, paused over, this last sentence. If you have training in some common-sense philosophy, be it existentialist or Anglo-Saxon, you may not take kindly to its claim. There may be a way out insofar as I might yield the name philosophy to whatever one might like to call philosophy, but still claim that there is a complex of contemporary problems which require the existence of a science of methodology in my sense.

I do not deny that methodology is already a contemporary concern. An introduction is no place to develop the view that that concern has not blossomed into wisdom. What I wish, rather, is to develop the empirical interest of the reader in the direction of herself or himself. The science in question is that of self-attentive methodology. That there is such a science is something I must gradually substantiate. Just as the common-sense attitude does not easily acknowledge the scientific horizon, so neither common sense nor science can easily acknowledge this further methodological horizon. Thus, the botanist's reaction to my claim that part of self-attentive methodology deals with the method of botany may be to say, "But surely I'm the man to deal with that: I have been doing botany for years and am extremely familiar with its method." And to convince him that familiarity with the method of botany is a far cry from the understanding of it given by methodology or metabotany is no easy task.

One way of leading the scientist, or the common-sense person, to some appreciation of the existence and nature of this science of methodology is to indicate the various problems of method that are present in contemporary culture. The difficulty of such indications, however, is that they can be appreciated only by the person engaged in the relevant field. Thus, there are basic methodological problems in contemporary physics, particularly in quantum mechanics and relativity, but for any reader who is not actually engaged in these fields, the existence of such problems will be a matter of belief. And even the quantum physicist may puzzle over my use of the expression "methodological problems." He will grant that there is obscurity about the relation of quantum theory to reality or about indeterminacy: but why "methodological"?

One may say that a problem of method is a problem of know-how or know-what-we're-doing. Putting the problem this way helps throw the stress where it should be: on the person doing the science and not on the science conceived of in some strange way as independent of mind. Now from this angle the problem in quantum theory would be expressed as "What-are-we-at in doing quantum mechanics?" To elaborate on that problem would be out of place here and probably meaningless for the ordinary reader: it is for the interested specialist to follow up the lead and re-express his problems in this mode.

But the problem of horizon haunts this interest and this re-expression. So, for example, John Hicks, in his comparative study of methods of dynamic economics, remarks of Erik Lindahl:

> Lindahl was himself quite a bit of a methodologist; he was fond of reflecting on what he himself was doing. He thus came to be perfectly conscious that it was a new dynamic method that he was devising. But that, of course, was after the event. The method would not have been devised because there was a methodologist's pigeonhole for it; it was devised because there was a need for it. The particular place where the need was felt—in Sweden, as in contemporary England—was in monetary economics.[5]

Now I do not question the achievements of either Hicks or Lindahl in economics. But my claim, frankly, amounts to asserting that they are only at the beginning of the descriptive phase of methodology in my sense. Both men have experience of economic understanding and, as Hicks notes, that experience makes possible the acknowledgment of changes in it, changes of method. But to name and describe a method or a change of method may be no nearer explanatory self-attentive methodology than descriptive classification in botany is to phylogenetic correlations. Let me illustrate the point further by considering the question, what is understanding?

Understanding may be briefly described as what is rare in the stupid and what occurs more frequently in the intelligent. But can we get beyond this description? Consider more closely the What-question, What is understanding? Let us compare it with other such questions, as What is a dog? What is light? These questions, too, can be answered descriptively and acceptably: the dog can be described in terms of evident shape and activities; light can be described in terms of color. But besides these descriptions there are sciences which deal with dogs and light. In them dogs and light are taken as data to be understood, and the understanding required constitutes respectively the sciences of zoology and physics. Comparing this with our question, What is understanding? the possibility of a parallel should not be too unacceptable. Our datum in this case is understanding, our own understanding. Just as the zoologist has experience of dogs so we have experience of our own acts of understanding. Just as the zoologist can center his attention on that experience of dogs, familiarize himself with all sorts of specimens and slowly grow in an understanding of animals and plants, so we may center our attention on our own acts of understanding, accumulate specimens from various fields, and slowly grow in an understanding of our understanding. There are, of course, professional philosophers who would deny that we could attend to ourselves and grow in an understanding of our understanding. But how do they reach this conclusion: by not attending to themselves, by not trying to understand themselves?

Again, while authority is not a popular source of proof, it is nice to know that great men are on our side. Neither Aquinas nor Aristotle had any doubts as to how to go about understanding the nature of intelligence:

> The species therefore of the thing actually understood is the species of the understanding itself; hence it is that understanding can understand itself through this species. Thus the philosopher in an earlier passage studied the nature of possible intellect by studying the very act of understanding and the object that is understood.[6]

One might recall, too, the Socratic stress on self-knowledge, Augustine's stress on introspection, Descartes's quest for method, and Kant's search for a science that should determine *a priori* the possibilities, principles, and extent of human knowledge.[7] In each there is an appreciation of, and a groping toward, knowledge of knowledge. Nearer our own times we have a tradition of interest in the existential subject running from Kierkegaard to Heidegger, but that interest never blossomed out into a genuine science of the subject. At the end of his big book on Heidegger, W. J. Richardson poses various questions and concludes, "But these are questions, questions, questions. Are there no answers to be had? What must we do to find them?"[8] While Richardson answers that last question with a quotation from Heidegger, "We must do nothing but wait," I prefer to recommend the self-attentive technique by which the subject, the reader, would get to grips with himself or herself in a novel and fundamental way. This getting to grips with oneself is no mean task, and there is the ever-present danger of abandoning it in favor of a mastery of the language of the new science. "As you know, mankind has an instinctive antipathy to intellectual novelties; one of the ways in which this shows itself is that any such novelty is immediately reduced to its very smallest compass, and if possible embodied in some catchword."[9] For this reason will be at pains throughout to keep the reader from the illusion that I am making a methodologist out of him or her. I offer only signposts, elementary directions, a grammar of procedure. I have been struggling with the science of self-attentive methodology for fifteen years now. Its fruits are as slow in coming forth as they are fundamental and significant personally and culturally.

The effort to understand one's own knowing can be related in another fashion to the history of philosophy, to the quest for wisdom which was focused by Aristotle. Every science has its history, its period of confusion and myth, its eventual emergence as a definite science. Before chemistry, there was alchemy, before astronomy there was astrology. So in philosophy. There is clear evidence that Aristotle, Augustine, and Aquinas all indulged in self-attentive understanding, but none of them elevated it into a scientific technique. That elevation is demanded by, and being realized in, our own times. The establishment of self-attentive technique marks a transition in philosophy analogous to the transition from alchemy to chemistry. The relation between self-attentive understanding and the results of such men as Aristotle will obviously not be clear to the reader from what has been said. But apart from that relation there is the radical view proposed, a view that can hardly expect, even if it were spelled out, wide acceptance: an essential transition in a science is always incredible to those long familiar with a prior stage, a prior view. As Max Planck put it, a new scientific position does not gain general acceptance by making opponents change their minds—it does so by holding its own until old age has retired them from their professional chairs.[10]

Again, one may see this transition on the broader canvas of history. Karl Jaspers places a basic axis of history in the period between 800 and 200 B.C. when man in some way came of age in Greece, in Persia, in Israel, in India, in China.[11] Later, in the context of a discussion of contemporary culture, he points to the needs of the contemporary scene and to the possibility of a new axis.[12] Might I suggest that there is something axial about the emergence of self-attentive methodology as a scientific technique?[13]

What are the fruits of that emergence? Two aspects immediately suggest themselves—one negative, the other positive. The negative aspect is not unrelated to Jasper's reflection:

> Wonder at the mystery is itself a fruitful act of understanding in that it affords a point of departure for further research. It may even be the goal of all understanding, since it means penetrating through the greatest possible amount of knowledge to authentic nescience, instead of

allowing Being to disappear by absolutizing it away into a self-enclosed object of cognition.[14]

The negative aspect is the reaching of authentic nescience. It is a common human failing to mistake eloquence for explanation and familiarity for understanding. Socrates' criticism was an effort to reveal to the Greeks that in a peculiar way they didn't know what they were talking about. Self-attentive understanding opens up the possibility of the reader's appreciating his own nescience within a new horizon. Such an appreciation is of enormous significance in our times when common sense is so meshed with common nonsense, when the human sciences are bandied about in popular parlance. And here one may move to the positive aspects of the fruit of methodology: for self-attentive methodology offers man the possibility of getting to grips with his meaning at its focus. Existentialism and historical consciousness have succeeded in underlining man's creativity of his own essence. That emergent essence is centrally on the level of mind, and the more man appreciates the nature of the emergence of meaning, the more adequately will he contribute creatively to that emergence. That appreciation will enable him to move from state of spontaneous use of his intelligence in his doing to a level of intelligent guidance of that use.[15]

This last point regarding the possibility of transition to intelligently guided use of intelligence in fact brings us right to the center of the contemporary problem in economic methodology. It is, however, far from the center of contemporary precise economic debate. As Heilbroner remarked in

> a brief glimpse at the state of contemporary methodology. It cannot be said that a passion for the subject is a mark of contemporary economics. Inquiries into the nature of economic theorizing, or into the relation between economic inquiry and science proper, are not only difficult to find these days, but when found rarely exhibit that zeal for exactitude so characteristic of other branches of contemporary economics.[16]

One trouble is that methodology of economics is not just another branch of economics: and that is precisely our trouble of horizons. But our immediate interest is in the preliminary ground-clearing without which discussions of the central issues can in fact be highly mythic. Here I would like to note my disagreement with such as Auguste Comte regarding progress in civilization. New words and new techniques only extend the scope of myth-makers and magicians, and radical existentialism, while it offers new meaning, also offers new words, new techniques. The elimination of the mythic about what is real or of value may become common in post-axial man, but the task of eliminating such myth will always be there, and will also, I suspect, be both difficult of achievement and surprising in its results.

> Unfortunately, some people have the impression that while Tertullian and others of his time may have made such a mistake, no one repeats it today. Nothing could be further from the truth. For until a person has made the personal discovery that he is making Tertullian's mistake all along the line, until he has gone through the crisis involved in overcoming one's spontaneous estimate of the real, and the fear of idealism involved in it, he is still thinking just as Tertullian did. It is not a sign that one is dumb or backward. St. Augustine was one of the most intelligent men in the whole Western tradition and one of the best proofs of his intelligence is in the fact that he himself discovered that for years he was unable to distinguish between what is a body and what is real.[17]

Let us, then, face the foothills of these next four chapters.

Notes

[1] J. Schumpeter, *Business Cycles*, New York and London, McGraw-Hill, 1939, vol. 1, 99.

[2] The cycles were named after economists associated with their investigation. The Juglar was somewhat over eight years long. A shorter cycle of about three years was named after the Englishman Kitchin. The Russian economist Kondratieff gave his name to the long cycle of about sixty years.

[3] See B. Lonergan, *Insight*, Longmans, 1957, 226 ff.; CWL 3, 251–261.

[4] P. McShane, "Zoology and the Future of Philosophers," *Horizons*, Dublin, Milltown Institute, Dublin, 1971; *The Shaping of the Foundations: Being at Home in the Transcendental Method*, Washington, University Press of America, 1976, 79–95.

[5] John Hicks, *Capitalism and Growth*, Oxford University Press, 1972, 58.

[6] From St. Thomas's commentary on Aristotle, *In III De Anima*, lect. 9, n. 724.

[7] *Critique of Pure Reason*, Introduction, section 3.

[8] *Heidegger: Through Phenomenology to Thought*, The Hague, Martinus Nijhoff, 1963, 641.

[9] S. Freud, *General Introduction to Psychoanalysis*, New York, Perma Books, 1953, 225.

[10] M. Planck, *Scientific Autobiography and Other Papers*, edited by F. Gaynor, New York, Philosophical Library, 1949, 33 ff.

[11] K. Jaspers, *The Origin and Goal of History*, London, Routledge and Kegan Paul, 1953, chapter I.

[12] *Op. cit.*, 97.

[13] See "An Interview with Fr. Bernard Lonergan S.J.," *Clergy Review*, LVI (1971), 428; CWL 13, 176–194.

[14] *Op. cit.*, 18.

[15] See B. Lonergan, *De Deo Trino, Pars Systematica*, Rome, 1964, Q. XXI, "*Quaenam sit analogia subjecti temporalis et subjecti aeterni*"; CWL 12, 399–413.

[16] Robert L. Heilbroner, *Between Capitalism and Socialism*, New York, Random House, 1970, 168.

[17] B. Lonergan, in a talk on "Consciousness and the Trinity," 1964 (unpublished); *Philosophical and Theological Papers 1958–1964*, vol. 6, Collected Works of Bernard Lonergan, Robert C. Croken, Frederick E. Crowe, and Robert Doran (eds.), Toronto, University of Toronto Press, 1996, pp. 122–141.

Chapter 2 ~ Pillars of Wisdom

I would advise none to read this work, unless such as are able and willing to meditate with me in earnest, to detach their minds from commerce with the senses, and likewise to deliver themselves from all prejudice.[1]

I could make Descartes's sentiments entirely mine were it not for the fact that I wish precisely that the reader engage in commerce with the senses. But I do require earnest meditation of a particular kind. And I do want prejudices left aside. By prejudices I mean particularly views of what philosophy is about, the meaning of different systems of philosophy which the reader might fancy to use as a term of comparison with what he or she expects to find here. I will not in fact be talking here about systems of philosophy. I will be talking about the reader, you, and asking you to attend to yourself, to ask yourself certain simple questions, to reach elementary answers.

First of all, I hope that the reader is conscious: not a vain hope, since if you were unconscious you would not be reading this book. Being conscious, of course, does not involve any type of looking at yourself. If you are looking at pictures in a gallery you are conscious: but that does not mean that there is an extra looking-at-yourself. Looking at pictures just happens to be that sort of activity which I call conscious. Again, you are intelligently conscious when you are puzzling over a problem: you are intelligently conscious, too, I hope, as you read this book, and since the approach is unfamiliar you are perhaps not a little puzzled. Are you?

The last question should halt you in your tracks. If you are willing to meditate with me in earnest, then you will have to settle down to some serious self-attention. Am I puzzled? The question is to be asked by the reader about herself or himself. Its answering requires attention to himself or herself on the part of the reader. Now, self-attention is not a matter of looking at oneself, as the reader will find if he or she continues with me. For that self-attention one may, indeed, sometimes use the word "introspection": but that is just an unfortunate limitation of language. At any rate I ask you to answer certain simple questions about yourself, and these questions and answers will involve some degree of what I call self-attention.

First of all, do you ever wonder? Are you perhaps even now wondering about what we are at and where it is all leading? If so, then you will be able to answer the first question affirmatively: Yes, I wonder about this and that, and I am wondering where all this is leading at the moment. So far, so good.

What, then, do you wonder about? For it would seem that you don't just wonder in a vacuum. You may wonder about a sudden noise, or about the meaning of a sentence in this book. You may wonder about many things but certainly you will admit that you have wondered on occasion about what you have seen or heard, etc., or even about something imagined. You might well at this moment imagine a rainbow—did you ever wonder about the rainbow and perhaps appeal to a physicist friend or a textbook in order to satisfy your wonder? Your wonder would be satisfied insofar as you reached some understanding of why the rainbow appeared as it did, one might say, of *what* a rainbow is. As we shall see better in the next chapter, Why- and What-questions are closely related. At any rate your basic question to your physicist friend would be some form of the question, What is a rainbow? It is, of course, to the physicist you go, for you expect him to understand light, and it is understanding you seek. When you yourself reach understanding you, too, will be able to explain: but before you understand you literally haven't an idea. In the present case what you are hoping to understand is the appearance of the rainbow, and depending on the pedagogical skill of your friend, your hope will not be in vain.

It is interesting in this context of trying to understand, or learn, or teach, to reflect on a famous passage in St. Thomas's *Summa Theologica:*

> Anyone can find in his own experience that, whenever he tries to understand anything, he forms phantasms for himself, to serve as examples in which he may—by inspection, as it were—reach that which he is striving to understand. And for the same reason, when we wish to make anyone understand anything, we offer him examples from which he can form phantasms for himself, in order to understand.[2]

One might well pause here to consider the importance and relevance at all levels of education of the pedagogical principles implicit here.

So far I have centered attention on wonder in one mode, wonder expressed in a What-question. That wonder, when satisfied, leaves one capable of defining or explaining. Now wonder expresses itself also in another mode: as an Is-question. Have you had experience of this mode? "I wonder if it is raining." "Is smoking injurious to health?" etc. Wonder expressed in this mode is satisfied by an intelligent "Yes" or "No," or even by a "Probably" or an "I don't know."

Next, you might consider how these two modes of wondering are related. While this might most easily be illustrated from science you might try reflecting on such, a simple illustration as being awakened during the night by a scraping sound. You may start by wondering what woke you up, but let us say that you have got to the stage of asking, What is that scraping? A mouse? Notice here that there is no problem in such a simple case of searching for definition: you already have some description of what a mouse is. But is it a mouse? Yes or No? The intelligent thing is to get up, put on the light and inspect the room. And so on. It is for the reader to multiply examples and thus to appreciate that he wonders, that that wonder is related to experience, that it operates in two modes.

We will be concerned in the following two chapters with each of these modes in turn. But before tackling them in more detail it is worthwhile to reflect on the universality of this structured wonder.[3] This structured wonder about experience, which you are discovering in yourself, is in fact something which you share with all men, be they of the present or the past, of the East or the West.[4] A classic debate in contemporary theology contrasts the mentality of the Hebrews and the Greeks. But in the light of their common sharing of structured wonder, that contrast reveals itself as not being fundamental. No doubt the Hebrews, unlike the Greeks, did not turn to a discussion of wonder or of questions. But they asked questions, and one has only to work through a random section of the Bible, picking out the question marks of a modern text, to appreciate that the questions are identifiably of two modes. What is true of the Bible is true also of the works of Mao Tse-tung or Marx or Adam Smith. What differentiates the questions and the answers and the cultures is a larger issue: But the point you are asked to note and reflect on is that common structure of questioning.

However, I will continually emphasize that the reader's primary concern is with himself or herself and his or her operations of inquiry.

I have written of structured wonder and I conclude this glare chapter with a diagram which indicates that structure. We will have to deal in turn with the elements and their interrelations as indicated, and so gradually reveal to ourselves—for I, too, learn even as I type—the significance of the pattern.[5]

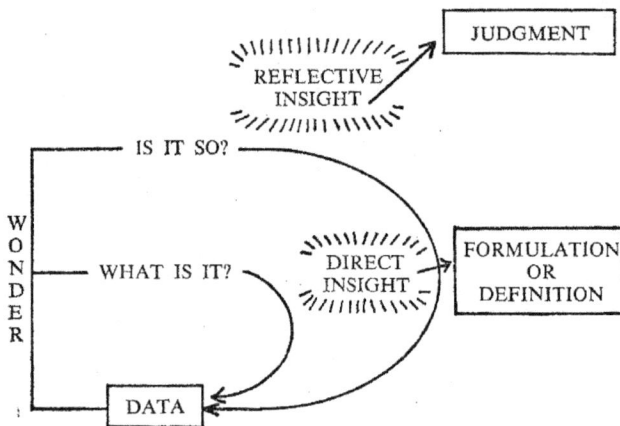

Structured Wonder

Notes

[1] R. Descartes, *A Discourse on Method*, London, Everyman's Library, 1953, 73.

[2] *Prima Pars*, q. 84, a. 7.

[3] You will note here the beginnings of a rejection of the relativism mentioned in the preface. It is of course a longer job to move to the precise position on historical knowledge and cultural conditionedness called perspectivism. See B. Lonergan, *Method in Theology*, Darton Longman and Todd, 1972, 217; CWL 14, 205.

[4] See F. E. Crowe, "Neither Jew nor Greek, but One Human Nature and Operation in All," *Philippine Studies* (13) 1965, 456–517; *Appropriating the Lonergan Idea*, ed. Michael Vertin, Washington, The Catholic University of America Press, 1989, pp. 31–50.

[5] The reader may have noticed that I have dodged some other types of question. We do spontaneously require, whether with a new house or an operating economic plan that it be a *reasonably realized possibility*. Some tricky self-questioning in regard to the questions leading to that demand would bring one to conceive, within interiority, of the classic final, efficient and exemplary causes. In this chapter, and through the book, our interest is restricted mainly to the questions relating to the other two classic causes, form and matter.

Chapter 3 ~ The What-Question

"What is that, Mammy?" asks the child visiting the zoo.

"A wallaby, dear," answers the mother, after a quick glance at the notice under the cage.

"What is a wallaby, Mammy?"

"That is, dear."

"Why, Mammy?"

There is no denying the native wonder of man. Years of faulty education and discouragement can undoubtedly quell that wonder. Pressure toward feats of memory, toward information rather than formation, can rush the adolescent past the effort genuinely to understand. A superficially sophisticated society can condition its young members into concentration on eloquence and a cloaking of any suspicion of radical nescience. A culture which should know better can leave unquestioned the illusion that, while man does not understand everything, still he has a jolly good idea.

A discussion of decadence and bias is well beyond our limited scope. In the conclusion to chapter six I will return briefly to these topics under the heading of personal authenticity and in chapter ten further dimensions will be touched on. Still, it is worth noting here that there are such problems and that they do not make any easier the task of appreciating the meaning of the What-question.

The visitor to the zoo can reach a certain contentment in being able to name the animals: Knowing a name somehow gives confidence, power. But knowing the name and being able to describe the animal is a far cry from understanding it—as Socrates revealed in his own way to his contemporaries. It is my hope here to lead the reader some distance toward Socratic wisdom, toward the wisdom of authentic nescience. I hope to bring you to appreciate the difference, the gap in question. We do anticipate by our native wonder an understanding of things great and small: but that anticipation can be psychically and culturally coupled with the illusions we have mentioned. Understanding of the use of words can pass for the understanding of what the words denote.

It is through this gap that there proudly march the speculative gnostic and the practical magician. They anticipate scientific understanding of what things are and how results are to be produced. They anticipate the pure scientist's preoccupation with numbers and the applied scientist's preoccupation with tools. They are necessary factors in the dialectical development of human intelligence, for without their appearance and their eventual failure, men would not learn the necessity of effective criteria for determining when adequate insight actually has occurred. But because their efforts are prior to the discovery of those criteria, because their pure desire to know is not contrasted with all other desires, because names and heuristic anticipations can be mistaken for insights, because partial insights have the same generic character as full understanding, because the satisfaction of understanding can be mimicked by an air of profundity, a glow of self-importance, a power to command respectful attention, because the attainment of insight is a hidden event and its content a secret that does not admit communication, because other men worship understanding but are not secure enough in their own possession of it to challenge mistaken claims, the magician and then the gnostic have their day.[1]

As one moves up the hierarchy of the human sciences one finds that the danger of such mythic thinking increases. In the sciences, from physics to zoology, such mythic thinking is not of course absent, especially when the scientist's speech touches on methodological issues. Again, the zoologist is liable to claim that he knows what a horse is more than the physicist is liable to make the same claim about the neutron. In the human scientist the liability of the zoologist blossoms into prevalent bias. But, further, a quite new level of intelligibility—the field of intelligible emanations to use a technical term—here becomes intrinsic to the object of study, and in this field core alienation gives rise to a dehumanizing neglect of meaning and method.

But let us leave this broad topic for the moment. I wish now to invite you to make an initial effort to appreciate the gap in question. But do not be deceived by the remoteness or "insignificance" of the illustration, the white magic of getting square roots. Besides techniques for getting square roots there are less white techniques for manipulating people.

Let us recall, then, the rule for extracting square roots which no doubt you learned in school. A simple illustration will serve:

```
            1 3 2
            ─────
  1         17424
            1
            ─
 23          74
             69
             ──
262          524
             524
             ───
```

You recall the rule? The number whose square root is sought is divided into pairs of numbers starting from the unit end. These pairs are "brought down" successively. Each time the number already reckoned, e.g., 13, is doubled and used to determine the next number in the square root, etc., etc. A little practice will refresh your memory and the process of getting square roots can become almost automatic. You can use the rule with ease. But our crucial question is, do you understand the rule, the *why* of it? What is *meant* by the procedure? You were taught how to use the rule at some stage, but it was not in fact explained. Indeed the explanation may well have been beyond your teacher.

To ask you to remedy that defect at this stage and age may seem very much beside the point. You had hopes perhaps of a panoramic view of the world and now, alas, you find the path to wisdom strewn with square roots! A panoramic view indeed there is, but it can only come at the end of a long climb. Here I can only indicate how you might go about the first hard steps.

But note that I am not just interested in getting you to remedy a defect in your mathematical education. I would hope that you would now engage not just in mathematics but in the methodology of mathematics. Let me enlarge on this point.

I have provided you with a puzzle: What is the meaning of this rule for extracting square roots, why does it work? Now I would like you to solve this puzzle but during the procedure to have a dual interest. For I wish you not only to be interested in solving the problem, but also to be interested in how you go about doing so. I want you to add to the puzzle the question, "How do I go about solving this puzzle?" You should have, in other words, a methodological interest in the procedure. You should be able to ask and answer such questions as: Am I conscious, wondering, using diagrams, adjusting diagrams (disposing the phantasm, Aquinas might say), getting clues, hints, little insights?

You may well at this stage read on, thus showing to yourself that like so many others you have suffered the standard failure in education, the failure to learn how to read. Insofar as you understand everything I am writing about, you have only to "read" to understand. Now you may well understand the rule for extracting square roots, but do you understand what I mean by a dual interest, by self-attentive metamathematics? Please try it then before going on. If the rule for extracting square roots is too obvious, then you should be in a position to manufacture a rule for cube roots, and if you are to such an extent familiar with mathematics you should, in fact, have no trouble in finding data for metamathematics.

Now that you have at least tried, if not succeeded, let us consider how understanding of the rule may have emerged. Why pair off the numbers? Why double the results each time? Let us perhaps reverse the process, square the result. How? By straight multiplication. No, let us dispose the image, let us spread it out: The answer, 132, can be broken down into $100 + 30 + 2$, so instead of writing $(132)^2$ we can write $(100 + 30 + 2)^2$. You may not have remembered how to expand that, but with a little juggling you can arrive at the result:

$$(100+30+2)^2 = 100^2+30^2+2^2+2.100.30 + 2.100.2 + 2.30.2.$$

A clue that you might have got at this stage would relate the multiple "2" of the expansion to the doubling of the results at each stage. Notice here how the illustration was chosen helpfully to the extent that 132 does not include a repetition of a number: This helps for identification in the expansion. But notice also that it would have been more helpful to have had an illustration without the occurrence of the number "2": for that "2" can be confused with the multiplying "2." All this is related to Aquinas's and Aristotle's notion of modifying the diagram, disposing the phantasm, and to the role of the pedagogue in "setting things up," so that the solution begins to "stare the pupil in the face."

Next I recast the expansion to help you (in case you have failed):

$$(100+30+2)^2 = 100^2+2.100.30+30^2+2.100.2+2.30.2+2^2$$
$$= 100^2+(2.100+30).30+(2.100+2.30+2).2$$
$$= 100^2+230.30+262.2.$$

You may not have caught on even now: But don't give up, and don't hide behind the claim that really mathematics was never your line (this pronouncement is often made as if ignorance of mathematics was a special social grace!). I appeal to you to try again. Insight is a very precious thing, and insight into little things can be extraordinarily significant.

If you have reached the understanding of this rule, then you can shift from arithmetic to algebra, generalize it, etc., above all you can explain it pedagogically to someone else.

And perhaps now you have some insight into the difference between the use of the rule and the meaning of the rule. The instance has been given on the level of mathematics, but it has its parallel in all other fields—it is for the reader to push that parallel. But especially it should be considered in the basic context of the use of words and the meaning of words.

One might reflect similarly on a variety of What-questions, What is acceleration? What is heat? What is malaria? What is neurosis? What is love? What is money? What is man? All along the line there is the possibility of identifying the nature and limitations of one's understanding. Let us double back our consideration on itself by noting that just as the taxi-driver may claim to know quite well what acceleration is, just as the non-zoologist may claim to know quite well what a dog is, just as the non-economist may claim to know what a bank is, so you may have tended to claim, till now, that you know quite well what understanding is. I am here concerned with bringing you to a rejection of that claim and to the beginnings of an understanding of your own understanding. The basic distinction is between experience or familiarity and understanding.[2] Undoubtedly you have had experience of understanding before now: But till now you perhaps never raised the question, what is understanding? in any serious sense.

I return to the more straightforward task of bringing you to appreciate the distinction between familiar experience and explanatory understanding. Again, I take a simple piece of mathematics—it is for you to reach into your own experience for other possible sources of enlightenment. You might consider that we would be better employed discussing more relevant instances of the distinction; for instance, that familiarity with people's faces is a far cry from understanding people. But you might agree too easily with this, you might too easily obscure the radical difference between experiencing, seeing, etc., and understanding. But note, as you go on to the mathematical problem, that the familiar faces of our friends are sometimes oval. If we do not understand the mathematics of a face, what of its meaning?

Consider, then, the familiar oval shape called an ellipse. What is an ellipse? You might answer: an oval shape, a plate looked at sideways, etc. But, like the child in the zoo, I might follow up with the question, Why? We are, in short, seeking for the law of the ellipse, if you like, how is it made? Following up this last suggestion I give you a clue—and don't forget that your interest is methodological—an ellipse has two centers: Try two of your fingers in a loop of thread.

There will be those, of course, who read on here without pausing, those who find this little book fascinating perhaps but beside the point. A pity: For I certainly would not foist such illustrations on the public did I not think that the self-appropriation that they might bring was enormously relevant in our times. I recall J. L. Synge's comment on Jacques Hadamard's little book on the psychology of mathematics:

> Such things may strike us strange and rather fascinating, a strand of queerness enlivening the dull desert of scientific thought, arid stretches of logic. We may dismiss them lightly and pass on to the serious consideration of what thought and understanding are in terms of the words that philosophers have been accustomed to use. But we may be quite wrong in this. We may miss the turning leading to an understanding of understanding.[3]

Returning to our ellipse, we find that the successful drawing leads to a definition of an ellipse: the locus of points such that the sum of their distance from the two fixed points remains constant. In symbols $AP + BP = Constant$, where A and B are fixed and P is a point on the locus. We have thus arrived at a What-answer. Is it correct? In asking that question I anticipate the next section, on the Is-question, and the reader will find it worthwhile to return to this passage when that section has been reflected upon. Now, in fact, the definition is not correct. Why? Recall that the coast of Ireland is the locus of points equidistant from a fixed point!

We could now possibly pause to spell out here what is so densely expressed in Lonergan's *Insight*, 7–12, but I would ask the reader to answer reflectively only the question, Can you imagine the definition of an ellipse? Is seeing anything like understanding? I would hope that the reader would gradually come to appreciate that there is no analogy whatever between perceiving and answering a question, be it a What-question or an Is-question.

The reader will notice that the definition of an ellipse is relational, and that the relations are, so to speak, of parts of the ellipse to each other.

Before reaching that definition I wrote of the ellipse in terms of how it looked to us. This illustrates a general characteristic of the shift to definition. Think of the question, What is pressure? The immediate answer will be in terms of push and pull. The answer in terms of the gas laws involves correlations of correlations of correlations. The repetition is deliberate. Do you recall the simple apparatus used? A volume of gas, a column of mercury, a ruler, etc.? Now a ruler already involves a first set of correlations—the reader should not take that for granted: It is an opportunity for wonder and insight into measurement, coupled with the possibility of self-attentive reflection. Then there are the sequences of measurements of volumes and pressures leading to a set of numbers such as:

$$P \quad 30 \ 40 \ 50 \ 60 \ 70 \ 80 \quad 90 \ . \ . \ . \ .$$
$$V \quad 12 \ 9 \ 7 \ 6 \ 5 \ 4\tfrac{1}{2} \ 4 \ . \ . \ . \ .$$

One reaches the law from the clue gained by multiplying and intelligently neglecting random differences, etc.

You are perhaps beginning to appreciate the flexibility and variability of insight, the manner in which intelligence can neglect just what is to be neglected and attend to what is relevant. No room here for some simpleminded view of abstraction: the modern world is a world of calculus, surds, limitation theorems in mathematical logic, psychic illness, and political unrest. Intelligence can comfortably do mathematics with a green pen and have no difficulty in excluding green from the definition. But the procedure can be trickier, and so, a long scientific education may be needed to control the spontaneous anticipation of understanding. If the fractions between 0 and 1 can be put in one-to-one correspondence with the natural numbers, then surely the decimals between 0 and 1 can be put in similar correspondence? Indeed, one might be inclined to say that the decimals might be easier to handle than the fractions. The problem here is to label the fractions—or decimals—so that for any given number the label can be produced, and vice versa. I might delay here to give hints, as in other examples, as to how to label the fractions. I go on immediately, however, to give a handy way of labeling all the positive rational numbers. The reader, of course, could profitably delay here and try for himself or herself.

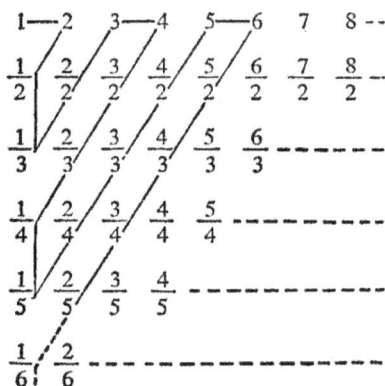

The trick is to lay out the rational numbers in a suitable array and then label them diagonal-wise as indicated in the diagram (there is a minor problem of leaving out the repeats). Now, you may name a rational number, I can find its label; you name a label, I'll point out its number.

Can we do the same for decimals? The simplest labeling would seem to be the following:

$$
\begin{array}{ll}
1. & .00000000000\dots\dots \\
2. & .10000000000\dots\dots \\
3. & .20000000000\dots\dots \\
4. & .30000000000\dots\dots
\end{array}
$$

etc., etc.

Still, a little reflection reveals flaws in this list (does it?). Let's try another strategy: what we might call the mirror image method in that we keep subtracting ones from the decimal "reversed." The beginnings of the list will help the reader to grasp what I mean:

$$
\begin{array}{ll}
1. & .99999999999\dots\dots \\
2. & .89999999999\dots\dots \\
3. & .79999999999\dots\dots \\
\multicolumn{2}{c}{\dots\dots\dots\dots\dots\dots\dots} \\
10. & .09999999999\dots\dots \\
11. & .98999999999\dots\dots
\end{array}
$$

We may not in fact be too happy with that either. But we need not despair. There must surely be some way of lining up the decimals with the natural numbers. To admit that there isn't or couldn't be is to admit a certain lunacy into mathematics as if there were more numbers than could be counted.

Let us assume that we have a suitable list, something like the two suggested. Now make a new decimal by taking the first number from the first decimal, the second from the second, and so on. Change each of these by, say, one. (The acute reader will note a problem here.) Now we have a new decimal which differs from all those in our supposed complete list. Something of an inverse insight!

One last instance of twisted insight may be both of interest and of profit. Aristotle did not discover statistical science. But let us see how he might have. Suppose he noted in his evening paper that Peripetes was killed by a falling slate in Athens. A week later Alcibiades is similarly killed and the event is noted by Aristotle. So he continues and begins to count: not in itself a very significant procedure, not apparently leading anywhere. Suppose at any rate that he ends up with the facts that in a sequence of months,

$$6\ 7\ 5\ 6\ 8\ 5\ 7\ 5\ 6$$

people had been killed by falling slates. As Kepler had the data on Mars before him for many years, so Aristotle might have had such a list before him for years. But the trick is, intelligent neglect of the random. The neglect leads to an understanding of the ideal, the average—here 6—about which the numbers oscillate. How obvious when it is explained! Yet it was not for centuries that the relevant insights occurred. That is the sort of thing that the slow, painfully slow, development of man's understanding involves. Nowadays statistical methods are commonplace in science. It is quite another thing to understand introspectively what statistical method is, how it differs from and complements classical method, etc.[4] Such an understanding hardly belongs to the first steps of methodology, so we come here to a suitably abrupt halt.

It might be expected that some illustrations of What-questions from economics could be profitably discussed. The fact is that such What-questions have a complexity which goes beyond the limits of an introduction which asks you to ask, What are What-questions? I can only hint at that complexity. Take for instance the question, "What is deficit government spending?" For the man in the street, it is a budget deficit and even, perhaps, his children's burden of a national debt. For the economist the words name partly a technique, partly a problem. For the metaeconomist there is the challenge of rooting out the presuppositions of the technique and the axial prerequisites of a larger solution.

So, for example, there is the excellent *A Primer on Government Spending*, by R. Heilbroner and Peter Bernstein[5] which tries brilliantly to give the man in the street a view from the economist's perch.[6] The initiate metaeconomist would find in it a challenge to discover the nature of key economic insights and, more remotely, to discover the presuppositions, with their deficiencies, in the basic approaches to this debated issue.[7] Only thus could the methodological complexity be revealed. Economists recognize that complexity and are somewhat at a loss even with the basic question – What is economics? – equivalently, the question—What am I doing when I am doing economics? "One is led to conclude that economics as a scientific discipline is still somewhat hanging in the air."[8]

One last point brings us to the end of this short introduction to the question of What-questions. If the reader will pause and reflect on our discussion so far, he may perhaps arrive at the suspicion that I have been cheating a little. In a certain sense he would be correct. In our early instances of What-questions we stressed correlations, properties if you like. But properties are always properties *of*. There is an insight involved here, which is, one might say, so spontaneous that it is regularly neglected if not worse. It is for instance neglected in the current debate about transubstantiation in Christian theology. It is the insight associated with the notion of thing, substance. I hesitate to venture into this delicate region with its demand for serious and prolonged self-attention. Perhaps, however, I may add a short fable which I have found both personally and pedagogically helpful. It is about a man called Jonah. Jonah wakes up lying on his back feeling sick. The place is pitch dark, smelly, damp. He feels with his hands the damp, mossy surface around him. He gets to his feet and the whole place sways about. He shines his pocket torch around: He is in some sort of cave, reddish-colored, with odd projections and pieces of bone around. Then it dawns on him … "I'm in a whale!" Now, note that the "dawning" added nothing to the data beyond the unity-identity-wholeness of one thing (we speak loosely—obviously it pulls in his understanding of whales).[9] Was his insight verified and how was it verified? Note that we think of many "things" as things. The Germans probably think of their spectacles as a thing, "meine Brille"; do you? You can think of a car as a thing: Is it? How do you know?

I might go on here to discuss the role of scientists in determining what are things, etc., etc., but I think it best to bring this rambling chapter to a close with our fable, in that way adding emphasis to the claim that I am strictly giving a survey of the foothills of self-attentive methodology, that there is no short or easy way up the slope.

Notes

[1] B. Lonergan, *Insight*, 542; CWL 3, 565–6. Relevant here is a reflection on post-systematic, post-scientific, etc., meanings: See Lonergan, *Method in Theology*, 303–305; CWL 14, 283–4.

[2] I am avoiding refinements here which would require a discussion of descriptive, explanatory, and heuristic concepts.

[3] J. L. Synge, *Science, Sense and Nonsense*, London, Cape, 1951, 112.

[4] Some detailed help on this may be found in my *Randomness, Statistics, and Emergence*, Dublin, Gill and Macmillan, and University of Notre Dame, 1971; second edition, Vancouver, Axial Publishing, 2021.

[5] New York, Random House, 1971.

[6] *Op. cit.*, 4, 8, 55.

[7] The deficiencies are not merely heuristic deficiencies but deficiencies in systematics and in models. There is, generally, in economics, the tricky problem of having the correct "common matter," to use an old Thomist tag: to not be trying to define a man without his bones, so to speak (See B. Lonergan, *Verbum: Word and Idea in Aquinas*, Notre Dame, 1967, 143–147; CWL 2, 154–58). Von Neumann's Turnpike Theorem tradition, for instance, is scarce on bones. Max Planck is reported to have said that he found economics too difficult: the difficulty could well be related to the differences in abstraction in physics and economics. Again, apart from the Marxist historical approach, a deductivist philosophy of science is all too dominant. More of this in chapter 10.

[8] T. C. Koopman's, *Three Essays on the State of Economic Science*, New York, McGraw-Hill, 1957, 142.

[9] The topic is discussed at some length in Lonergan, *Insight*, chapter 8.

Chapter 4 ~ The Is-Question

Guilty or not guilty: That question does not ask for a definition, but for a verdict, a Yes or a No. No doubt when the jury retires to consider the case many of them may not be at all clear on the evidence. As they debate the issue among themselves, they come to understand better the events and circumstances, the motives and the opportunities. But there comes that stage when questions about the nature of the case yield to that attitude of mind which seeks to bring forth judgment: Guilty? Yes or No?

The jury retires to the jury room precisely to bring forth a judgment of this type. Judgment rests with them and they appreciate the responsibility and the element of personal commitment involved. They are selected as intelligent and unbiased, and their judgment is eventually accepted as fitting the facts, as strictly objective. They do not decide in the strict sense of that word that the person is guilty or not: The judgment of guilt directly relates to what actually happened, not to what they would like to have happened. Moreover, the happening includes not just external activities and circumstances, but such intangible elements as motives and sanity. Judgment, then, is not just a matter of looking in some mysterious way at the facts, what happened. It is, as it were, removed from the visible, the audible, the appearances. It lies within intelligence, within an understanding of the case in all its aspects, and when each jury member commits himself on the case he does so with the detachment of intelligence, with a nod of the head rather than a pointing of the finger. This last opposition, if you like, brings out the difference between answering a question and perceiving: there is no parallel between these. Again, the juror expects his judgment to be respected. To challenge a man's judgment is to come near to the bone. As de la Rochefoucauld says, "Everybody complains of his memory, but nobody of his judgment."[1] One often hears the remark, "I have a very poor memory," but rarely are we tempted to say, "I have a very poor judgment."

It is worthwhile reflecting on the odd statement that a judgment is invisible. It may be about appearances, but it is not an appearance. It has the remoteness of understanding from appearances. As earlier I pointed out that one cannot imagine the definition of a circle or an ellipse, so here I note that judgment is no more imaginable. Judgment, and the truth reached in judgment, is in people's minds and in people's minds only. I may express my judgment in a written sentence, but the written sentence is not true or false. The writing of itself is just a series of marks on paper—both the meaning and the truth are in my mind. One might find it helpful to consider the old paradox of the written sentence, "This sentence is false." Is it? If it is, then it is true, and vice versa. Again one might consider the question of judgment in relation to the truths in the Bible or in the Koran. In what sense are there truths in such sacred books? Certainly not in the sense that between any two of the dots that we call full stops there lies a truth. Truth, the fruit of judgment, is found only in a mind.

The procedure in the jury room in coming to judgment has the same generic structure as the procedure in a science of verifying some theory, some hypothesis. In both cases one moves from data to some understanding of the data which must be adequately checked. To understand the nature of that checking is to understand the nature of judgment or verification.

It is clear enough both from the illustration of the jury and from our previous considerations of the What-question about experience, that judgment somehow depends on these other levels and completes them. One cannot ask an intelligent Is-question without having a What-answer. "Is the kettle boiling?" requires, if it is to be answered, that the person questioned understands by his common sense what a kettle is, what "boiling" means. Indeed, it requires a lot more: The question may have arisen from hearing a whistling in the kitchen, and the answering comes through a use of many habits of understanding and behavior which we scarcely notice. In the general case one can say that judgment requires a background of other knowledge and understanding. Is this not the reason why we call in the expert? We go to the doctor that he may judge our health and our sickness and, of course, that we may be cured. We may be very sick but feeling sick and understanding the sickness are two radically different things. So we may go to the doctor and ask, for example, "Is it arthritis, doctor?" We have some vague notion of the connection between arthritis and stiffness, but it is the doctor who is in a position to judge, for he understands to some extent the symptoms of arthritis. To judge, of course, he must look, listen, etc., but the doctor's looking is very different from the patient's looking. It is backed by understanding. Again, the physicist trying to verify some elaborate theory may end up looking at a dial—but it is the significance of the place of the needle on the dial that is important. One might consider similar judgments regarding the economy, judgments regarding price control, or Is-questions such as, "Is non-inflation compatible with full employment?"

As yet, however, we have not tackled directly the question, What is a judgment? I may say immediately, of course, that it can be tackled only by the same method as is used in tackling the What-question. Judgment is something that occurs in us regularly. To answer the question, "What is judgment?" requires that we turn serious attention to that type of occurrence in ourselves. So far I have been indicating the role of intelligence in judgment in a general and familiar way. But it is quite another matter, indeed a matter of years of effort, to proceed self-attentively to an understanding of the reflective insight which gives rise to the answer to the Is-question. Do I exaggerate? Recall the conclusion of chapter 1 and cast an eye forward to my concluding remarks in chapter 5. Early in chapter 1 I mentioned the difference in the matter of apology between physics and self-attentive methodology. Mathematical physicists have put years of effort into investigating the self-energy of the electron. The elusive self-energy of questioning is a trickier and larger field. The problem of a possible infinity of electron self-energy is a piece of twentieth-century physics. The problem of a possible infinity of questioning-self-energy is the centerpiece of human history.

My problem here of course is to stir your curiosity about your own activity of judging to sufficiently serious dimensions to bring you to face the drab beginnings. One does not begin physics with Quantum Electrodynamics—one begins with rather unexciting Newtonian problems.

Let us return, then, to the jury room. The evidence has been heard. The evidence has been understood. At this stage the central interest of the jury is the question, "Is the evidence sufficient?" The basic problem is to grasp the sufficiency of the evidence—or its insufficiency. So the jury engages in weighing the evidence. But what do we mean by weighing the evidence? This is one of the problems facing us if we are to understand the reflective insight which gives rise to judgment.

Now, as I continually emphasize, there is little hope of readers reaching any worthwhile appreciation of that insight unless they are willing to attend to themselves in the specimens of their own significant judgments. By significant judgments I mean judgments which are not just imaginary, vague considerations of general sentences, etc. To be significant a judgment does not need to be elaborate or complicated. The question, "Is the door behind me open?" can be significant. If you raise that question—how it is raised is another matter—you react in a certain way to reach the answer, Yes or No. You look around. You see. But if you attend to yourself you will notice that the looking round was done intelligently: A dog, if asked the same question, might just wag his tail. Again, the seeing was intelligent. No doubt mere seeing was part of the judging, but the center of the stage was occupied by intelligence. What leads to judgment, "It is closed," is not mere seeing, but the grasp of the sufficiency of the seeing. Undoubtedly that may seem odd to more than a few. After all, you may only have to look! On the other hand, it may not seem at all odd to you. The next chapter will, I hope, help to undermine either view.

It is, at any rate, judgments of this type that I would like you to reflect upon initially—judgments, that is, concerning simple matters of fact. "Is the wind from the north?" "Is there a chance of recovery?" Questions like these give rise to such judgments of fact. You may profitably reflect on these questions in another form, thus bringing out clearly a certain aspect of judgment: "The wind is from the north?" "There is a chance of recovery?" One may note immediately that the transition to judgment consists, in some way, in merely removing the question mark. The defining meaning is already there: Yes or No adds nothing to it. The transition, I say, is effected by the grasp of the sufficiency of the evidence, an intelligent grasp which satisfies the wonder expressed in the question. But what is this grasp, and what does it grasp?

Consider again the question, "The wind is from the north?" To eliminate the question mark one might well go out, face a known direction and put a wet finger in the air. Why? Because these activities are intelligently appreciated as being relevant to the removal of the question mark. They are grasped, one might say, as conditions which if fulfilled will lead to the intelligent removal of the question mark, to the assertion "The wind is from the north." First we grasp the prospective judgment, but we grasp also conditions for its assertion and their link with the prospective judgment, and we seek to grasp their actual fulfillment.

Now it is important to note that the conditions are not like premises from which one deduced the required judgment. The conditions invariably involve a return to data which is neither judgment nor understanding. The cold feeling on one side of a wet finger is not a judgment but a feeling, about which no doubt we judge easily. And the prospective judgment does in fact involve such easy judgments as this. But as one pushes the issue back, say, to the question, "Is the far side of my finger cold?" one comes closer to appreciating the manner in which the conditions involve mere data.

Moving, then, from the Is-question to the judgment involves grasping the link between the prospective judgment and its conditions, some of which will be sensible, visible, audible, etc., and further, the grasping of the fulfillment of these conditions. The procedure may be formulated as follows:

If my raised wet finger feels colder on the north side; then the wind is from
    the north,
But my raised wet finger feels colder on the north side;
Therefore the wind is from the north.

The major premise here expresses an understanding of the link between
the prospective judgment and a sufficient condition; the minor premise
expresses the grasp of the fulfillment of that condition. The minor premise here,
of course, expresses another judgment: On this I have already commented. But
in the more basic case, the fulfillment of the conditions is appreciated in a
prejudgmental fashion leading, as was noted, to the elimination of the question
mark from the prospective judgment. If there were not such prejudgmental
grasp of the fulfilled conditions on the level of the given, data, we would land
in the problem of infinite regress. Thus, the minor premise above would require
another minor premise, X, in a new syllogism:

If X, then my raised wet finger feels colder on the north side,
And X,
Therefore my raised wet finger feels colder on the north side. And so *ad*
    infinitum.

However, concluding to the existence of prejudgmental insight into
fulfilling conditions, etc., does not rest on an argument such as this: it rests on
the experience of such insight in ourselves. It is for the reader to engage in that
experience with various judgments and to endeavor to understand its nature. It
is only by going over and over the process self-attentively that such
understanding can be reached. The illustrations I have taken have been simple
judgments of fact, but the reader may venture into more difficult judgments
such as judgments of science or history, to find the same basic structure and
further complexities.

A simple comment which may save the reader a variety of apparent
difficulties concerns the little word "is." The occurrence of this little word in a
sentence does not always connote a factual judgment: It occurs also regularly in
definitions such as, "A dog is an animal." The "is" in such definitions is, so to
speak, synthetic, holding-together. It can be clearly distinguished from the "is"
which occurs in judgments such as, "This dog is dead." In factual judgment the
"is" is associated with positing or rejecting, with saying what in fact is the real
state of affairs.[2]

Again, the reader may raise the question of the certainty of particular judgments. It is a question of interest and importance but could at this elementary stage be a source of confusion and distraction. Let me remark then that human certainty is not a black and white affair—nor, indeed, an affair of three degrees, moral certainty, physical certainty, and metaphysical certainty. Certainty, in fact, is a spectrum affair: How certain am I? Certain enough in a given case, less certain in another. In this connection one may mention that there is difficulty concerning the use of the word "probability" in relation to judgment. When we say that our judgment is probably correct, we express the fact that the content of the judgment is not quite as unconditioned as would be the case in a certain judgment. The fulfillment of the conditions may be problematic: "He is probably still in his office—at least he was when I phoned a few minutes ago." Probability in this sense, like certainty, refers to the content. There is on the other hand the probability which I touched on earlier by way of illustration of insight. That probability is a ratio, frequency, and it, is clearly distinguishable from the probability of a judgment. Like the difficulty with "is," this difficulty can be summarily dispatched by noting the relation of the two senses of probability to the two levels of cognitional structure: frequency-probability belongs primarily to the second level as content of a theory; probability of judgment belongs to the third level as quality of its content.[3]

Finally, if the reader investigates further the jury coming to judgment, he will appreciate that their judgment is not merely a matter of their own experience and understanding. They have listened to witnesses, reliable and less reliable. They have accepted evidence and other people's judgments on certain matters. In a word, their judgment is meshed with a complex of beliefs. Now judgment is one way of possessing the truth, belief is another and complementary way. In this section we have been raising in an elementary way the question, What is judgment? It is another and more difficult matter to face the problem, What is belief? We will return to it in chapter seven.

I hope I am not too tiresome in concluding with the remark that even if you spend a solid month on this chapter's suggested specimens, it is only a beginning. A month on the specimens of a major branch of botany or zoology would not have got you very far.

Notes

[1] *Maxims*, translated by L. W. Rancock, Penguin, 1967, Maxim 89.

[2] I am dodging here the issue of analytic propositions and analytic principles. See *Insight*, 304 ff; CWL 3, 329–34.

[3] I have discussed this topic more elaborately in *Randomness, Statistics, and Emergence*, Gill Macmillan and Notre Dame, 1970, 131–148; Axial Publishing, 2021, 109–122.

Chapter 5 ~ The Inside-Out of Radical Existentialism

What is the environment? The answer to this question comes promptly enough—the environment is "out there." It is this book, the walls of this room, the people passing to and fro; it is everything that is outside of us. This answer is of course a rational one, but it is founded upon an elaborate system of inferences developed through a lifetime of experiencing. If a forefinger **is** placed along the lower ridge of the eyesocket so that its tip is against the nose and the other eye is covered, pressing the eyeball gently and moving it up and down will cause the environment to jump back and forth. Now this is manifestly unreasonable! Any force sufficient to shake the room would also have been felt as vibration. But what, then, is the explanation of this phenomenon?[1]

The author goes on to give his explanation of this phenomenon which summarily is given in the remark that behaviorally, the environment is a pattern of neural energies in the central nervous system. I am not here embarking on an excursus into experimental psychology, though indeed one might well draw on its findings to strengthen the pedagogical strategy. But I am centrally interested here in that basic question, "What is the environment?" and this first illustration that Osgood gives of rocking the room may help the reader to rock that spontaneous conviction that reality is "out there." For I suspect that even though you have followed my arguments and illustrations so far, you may well have missed a central point, what I like to call the Bridge of Asses in methodology. You may well insist on agreeing with me that correct, verified understanding is knowledge of what is real and still be firm in the conviction that what is real is what is "out there." And so, let us here try to correct that view, by illustration and illusion, by parable and paradox.

Let me put the matter this way. Till now I have been describing and sketchily explaining a particular type of human activity called knowing. I have tried to get you to establish that there are three basic components, that the process of knowing is a three-storied process. Now this activity is going on in you, the organism. A diagram will help, but please remember that it is only a diagram, a crutch, to help you to understand yourself. Again, many of my remarks are of the same type—twisted truths, efforts to bring you through difficult insights: To take them out of that context and use them for philosophic mud-slinging would be to miss the point. The diagram on the next page represents you, the organism. I have put a three-floored box inside to indicate the activity of knowing, which we have discussed in the previous chapters. We might compare that activity to a process of digestion. What is being digested? Might I suggest the environment? In fact, I represent the sensitive integration by the lower box. W and the arrow indicate the "enzyme" wonder and its driving toward judgment through the What- and Is-questions. To complete the description of the diagram there are the two bumps on the organism to represent the eyeballs. Certainly there are many and varied receptors on and in the organism, but I find it convenient to concentrate my attack on the odd view of realism with which I associate the name "myth of the eyeballs."

Now if the reader will indulge in the experiment suggested in the quotation from Osgood, he or she will find that the environment rocks. I ask you to attend to that experience and to overcome the tendency to claim that obviously the real room isn't rocking but the appearances are disturbed. That of course is one of my twisted suggestions! What I am trying to counteract is the tendency to deny that the rocking is "out there." The rocking is, I hope you agree, very definitely "out there."

A parallel experiment consists in taking off your spectacles, if you wear spectacles, or putting on someone else's, if you don't. In that case the environment gets hazy. Again, I ask you to attend.

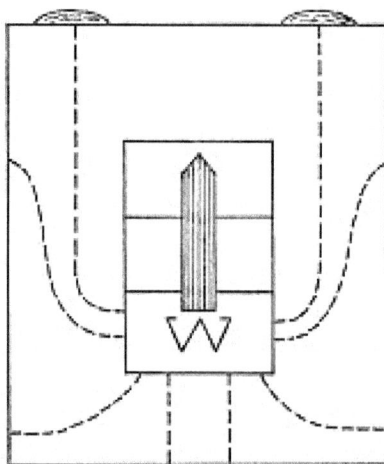

The Human Organism

36

You are looking at, say, legible print on distant book titles. You remove or put on spectacles—and the print gets hazy: what is hazy is what is "out there." One might say that the organism is such that what is represented by the bottom box in the diagram, the sensitive integration, has an extrojected quality, providing an environment for the animal. Let us try some logic on it. Obviously, the spectacles do not' affect anything beyond the lenses: It is only when the light hits the lens on its path to the eye that it is turned off its tracks. Then the logic is simple:

What the spectacles affect is not beyond the lenses;
What the spectacles affect is the "out there" environment;
Therefore the "out there" environment is not beyond the lenses.

Am I beginning to shake your sense of reality? You may feel that I am leading you into a strange subjectivism, that I am confining you within your own skin. Indeed, I am confining you within your own skin. To quote Tennessee Williams, "We are all condemned to solitary confinement within our own skins." At any rate insofar as you do not like my efforts you will argue against them, you will explain away my illustrations. Now in getting you thus to argue I consider that I have in fact boxed you in thoroughly. Let me explain this by first making clearer my own position.

My own position rests on a fundamental assumption: that what is real is reached by correctly understanding experience. [2] Correctly understanding experience is a process that goes on in the human organism. Its final fruit I may call the known. I assume an identity between the known and the real. Now obviously that identity is not ontological: knowing a cow is not having a cow in the mind. The identity is technically called intentional. But this is not the important point for you: The important point is to appreciate that there is no way whatsoever of comparing your activity of knowing to a reality known. As if, you might say, there was some possibility of a super-look, of getting outside your own skin!

The nice thing about my assumption is that it is inescapable. Certainly, you can't argue your way out of it without assuming it. For what is argument but the assumption that it is correct understanding that wins the day! Many philosophers have produced various and curious views of what is real and what is not: but they would all insist that their views were intelligent and reasonable and squared with what was given. With this in mind, you may return now to the task of arguing your way out of the view given above. Negatively expressed, that view denies that the environment "out there" is the real; positively expressed, it claims that the real is what is reached by, correctly understanding experience. Experience is a component, only a component of knowing.

Now you may well be with me all the way and still be inclined to claim that the known is in some way *like* the experienced, the environment "out there." No: the known is not similar to the "out there." You moved toward admitting this, indeed, when you conceded in chapter three that you couldn't imagine the definition of the ellipse. The real is no more imaginable. The known elephant is not *like* the seen elephant; and the real elephant is the known elephant (or to-be-known elephant, of course!).

We are here back at the difficulty mentioned at the end of chapter one, the difficulty of "the discovery (and one has not made it yet if one has no clear memory of its startling strangeness)"[3] that leaves idealism as a half-way house between materialism and radical existentialism. Moreover—and this is a point I return to in chapter ten—I refer to Lonergan here not as an authority, but precisely as a discoverer. "One has not only to read *Insight* but also to discover oneself in oneself."[4] The discovery is of radical heuristic self-discovery as the key to the philosophic quest, and the invitation is not "follow me" but "find yourself." What I wish to emphasize here, as I did at the end of chapter one, is the difficulty of this first step. It is a step not even commonly envisaged within contemporary philosophic communities. Perhaps of no other step in philosophy is the remark of Coleridge—a patient student of Kant—more true:

> But it is time to tell the truth; though it requires some courage to avow it in an age and country, in which disquisition on all subjects, not privileged to adopt technical terms or scientific symbols, must be addressed to the public. I say, then, that it is neither possible nor necessary for all men, nor for many, to be philosophers.[5]

I wrote in the preface of non-alienating self-justification. Here we are at its focus.

> Now because the third level is self-authenticating, reason and its ideal, the unconditioned, cannot be left in the dubious and merely supervisory role assigned them by Kant. Because it is constitutive and alone decisive, the one criterion in our knowledge is rational judgment; and this rules out the vestigial empiricism so often denounced in Kantian thought.[6]

The step I am inviting you to take is a giant stride in self-possession. It is not a step of belief but of self-understanding. Still, it does help and encourage perseverance in one's efforts of self-understanding believe that the step is there. These last chapters and this small book aid, I hope, in fostering both the belief and the beginnings of self-understanding. Like Augustine, you will take time to appreciate the oddities of sensibility. And you must go beyond Augustine's insight to come **to** understand what Aquinas spoke of as the light of intellect, what I named earlier the self-energy of questioning, in yourself. There is no escaping shades of sensible metaphor, but it is for you to get to grips with that inner is-saying in yourself, to slowly come to grasp the nature of that intimate activity of yours which is your capacity to *become* and to *be* all things. In the epilogue I use the word "outgoing" in an effort to describe *meaning*,[7] and judging is an act of meaning. But "outgoing" is a metaphor. Judging is "within" and the epistemological issue has nothing to do with getting out.[8] The simple startling fact is that it is the nature of your understanding to *be* an inner world which "intentionally" is the real world.

I resist the temptation to continue writing here of this simple' fact and its elusive appreciation. The step you are invited to take is one which is beyond the traditions of Kant or Hegel, American, Indian, or Chinese philosophy. Still, the invitation is there, and if you have experience of the growing challenge within contemporary science, history, or criticism, you will find that the accepted invitation brings slow clarity where the neglected challenge leaves obscure discomfort. I may quote Schumpeter here, agreeing certainly with his initial point that economics is not the place to handle the issue, but noting that what he adds only expresses the obscure discomfort of not facing the issue somewhere:

> We cannot enter here into the epistemological problem of the relation between "theory" and "facts" . . . The framing of hypotheses, although sometimes as necessary in our science as it is in all others, is neither the sole nor the main function of theory. If we are to speak about price levels and to devise methods of measuring them, we must know what a price level is. If we are to observe demand we must have a precise concept of its elasticity. No hypotheses enter into such concepts, which simply embody methods of description and measurement . . . and yet their framing is the chief task of theory, in economics as elsewhere.[9]

Commenting on the book from which. I have just quoted Heilbroner remarked: "Schumpeter is interested in discovering the subterranean forces that were at work."[10] Just before this Heilbroner had remarked on the abstractness of economics and continues: "By abstractness, I most emphatically do not mean dullness, for economics is anything but dull. I mean that the matters with which economics is concerned—inflation, poverty, even racism—undergo a curious fading as they come under the economic lens."[11] But what is the lens, and where are the subterranean forces? What is abstraction? What are hypotheses? Are theories real? What is real? What is not real? What is the real? May I suggest, and it is not just a criticism of Heilbroner, whose work I obviously admire, that we cannot afford to drift on into the twenty-first century without facing these issues, without digging out these assets.

Newman's thesis regarding theology in *The Idea of a University* may not claim much contemporary interest, but the issues mentioned here clamor for secular attention. Nor, I think, can academic life survive wholesomely without a personalist methodological concern which faces these questions at a level going beyond departmental exchange.

But this is a larger question. My present interest is in your engagement. You will, I hope, return to this chapter, or rather return to yourself in the manner suggested here. Meanwhile I invite you to investigate further dimensions of yourself such as that very evaluation and decision which would bring you back to this chapter.

I conclude with a quotation which neatly recalls the first quotation of this chapter and answers the question posed there, but within a wider context:

> A useful preliminary is to note that animals know, not merely phenomena, but things: dogs know their masters, bones, other dogs, and not merely the appearance of these things. Now this sensitive integration of sensible data also exists in the human animal and even in the human philosopher. Take it as knowledge of reality, and there results the secular contrast between the solid sense of reality and the bloodless categories of the mind. Accept the sense of reality as criterion of reality, and you are a materialist, sensist, positivist, pragmatist, sentimentalist, and so on, as you please. Accept reason as a criteriot etain the sense of reality as what gives meaning to the term "real," and you are an idealist; for, like the sense of reality, the reality defined by it is non-rational. In so far as I grasp it, the Thomist position is the clear-headed third position: reason is the criterion and, as well, it is reason—not the sense of reality—that gives meaning to the term "real." The real is what is; and "what is" is known in the rational act, judgment.[12]

Notes

[1] Charles E. Osgood, *Method and Theory in Experimental Psychology*, New York, Oxford University Press, 1953, 1.

[2] One may appreciate the introductory nature of this present treatment by comparing it to the movement of the book *Insight*. There, the invitation to appreciate the structure of one's knowing is issued in Part 1. The movement toward the fundamental assumption begins with Part 2 and has its climax on p. 388; CWL 3, 413. See the epilogue, endnote 21.

[3] B. Lonergan, *Insight*, xxviii; CWL 3, 22.

[4] B. Lonergan, *Method in Theology*, Darton Longman & Todd, 1972, 260; CWL 14, 244.

[5] S. Coleridge, *Biographia Literaria*, in the Chapter of Requests.

[6] B. Lonergan, *Insight*, 2nd edition, 341; CWL 3, 364. The change from the first edition adds a precision countering incomprehension, expressed in reviews, of his left-wing realism.

[7] I avoid the complex issue of the meaning of meaning in this short work.

[8] See B. Lonergan, *Insight*, 377; CWL 3, 401–2.

[9] J. Schumpeter, *Business Cycles*, New York and London, McGraw Hill, 1939, Vol. I, 31.

[10] R. Heilbroner, *The Economic Problem*, New Jersey, Prentice-Hall, 1972, xix.

[11] Ibid.

[12] B. Lonergan, *Verbum: Word and Idea in Aquinas*, University of Notre Dame Press, 1967, 7; CWL 2, 20.

Chapter 6 ~ Metaethics

I s capitalism to survive? Or socialism? Or is there possibly another way reaching back to the roots of both in eighteenth century innovation which yet could carry forward the benefits of technoassets in a new level of ascent?

These are large questions, and they will be posed again in a wider context in chapter ten and the epilogue. But our immediate interest in them is precisely as question-types. Whether or not these particular questions are yours, here and now, the question-types are the life-blood of your living. My modest hope here is to introduce you to an area of inquiry in yourself which yet is ultimately coterminous with all the dimensions of decision and desire. So I will be satisfied if I bring you to begin to grasp in your own decisions and doings a recurrence of the three levels already discussed, but now in a new context or with the addition of a new dimension. That new dimension is indicated in the accompanying diagram by the addition of a single line to the diagram at the end of chapter two. That single line denotes human will and willingness—your will of course—and the change in question-type denotes that we are dealing with what we call the pattern of concern.

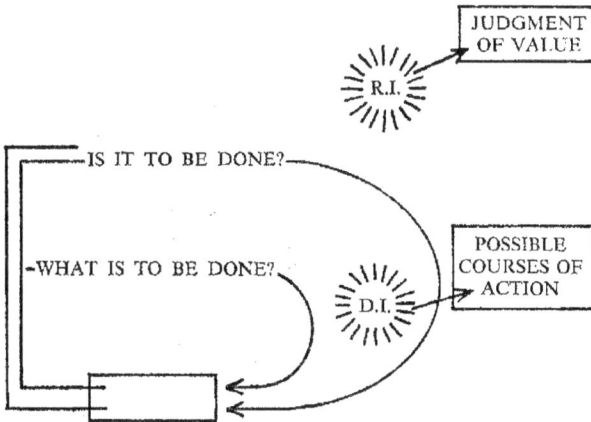

The Pattern of Concern

This pattern of concern occurs when we are up and doing, or about to be so. It is not to be confused with anxiety, any more than its opposite, complacency, is to be confused with laziness. Both "complacency" and "concern" are in fact technical words.[1] The meaning of "complacency" is perhaps best got at by reflecting on quiet enjoyment: for example, when one is enjoying a good non-aggressive film, a good book. It is an "all's well" attitude. It is easier to reach some notion of "concern," for it occurs when we are up and doing. It represents a "What's-to-be-done?" attitude. Now a "What's-to-be-done?" attitude, to be wholesome, must be based on a fundamental complacency, a *consent to being*, to the given state of affairs as a starting point. When it is not wholesome—as it is not, for example, in certain existentialist patterns of thought—then concern topples over into anxiety, *Angst, angoisse*.[2] Here I am briefly noting the significance of self-attentive understanding of human will for the restoration of a balance in contemporary culture. The reader might well consider a parallel in the opposition of insight and intelligibility to the cult of the absurd.

But let us return to our more elementary task of attending to ourselves in the pattern of concern. So far that pattern had not been mentioned, but this was by way of simplification. Human knowing and willing is not just a solid step-by-step process from experience to understanding to judgment to complacency to concern. There are, rather, "rapid oscillations" within the structure. But let me persist in my simplification—it is for the reader to self-attend to more complex patterns.[3]

Let us consider then a simple switch from a pattern of complacency to one of concern. You are driving along a pleasant country road with appropriate breeze and sunshine, and a tire blows. This is a distinct change of pattern, of attitude. Wonder enters a new phase: but it is still your same wonder with its same two basic expressions in What- and Is-questions. When you have taken in the situation your dominant question is, "What's to be done?" The answer to that question will regularly be a set of possible modes of operation: so, one could walk back to the garage passed earlier, or one could set to work oneself, and so on. Like all What-answers, these are the result of insight, and very clearly insight into the given situation, backed by one's habitual understanding. But what possible course of action is to follow? That is another question, which in respect to any possible course of action may be phrased, "Is it to be done?"

Continually here, I remind you to self-attend in examples of such questions. It is all too easy to read on, to miss the point. The point is that I am trying to draw your attention to your own experience of decision, that you may wonder about its nature, begin to understand it. Now the question, "Is it to be done?" is very near the focus of decision. "Is such and such a possible course of action to be realized by me here and now?" That is a question demanding reflective insight. Insofar as the required insight occurs and results in a Yes, then, insofar as one is reasonable, the decision follows, one is on the move. The decision, of course, does not always follow, but that failure is not something to be explained. Failure in decision is failure to be reasonable, and attempts to explain that unreasonableness are attempts to put reason where there is none. Such attempts normally are called rationalizations.

If the reader suspects that we are in an unusually difficult region here, he or she is correct. Self-attentive understanding of the will is a delicate operation and the region of methodology dealing with it is in its infancy. But as I noted in chapter one regarding Aquinas's program for understanding understanding here I note that the parallel program for understanding the will was not unknown to him. In an article of the *Summa Theologica* entitled "Whether the Intellect Understands the Act of Will" he concludes by programming that investigation: "And so the philosopher can say, 'the will is in the reason.' Now, if something is present intelligibly in an intelligent being it follows that it is understood by that intelligent being. Therefore, the act of the will is understood by the intellect inasmuch as (a) one perceives *that* one wills, (b) one knows the nature of that act and subsequently (c) the nature of its principle which is the habit or potency."[4] The reader interested in pushing forward with that program would find helpful data in the works of F. E. Crowe.[5] Here, as usual, I can only give random hints.

The most important point to reflect on perhaps is the difference between the simple Is-question and the Is-it-to-be-done question. The difference may be expressed as a difference of context: one's interest has been expanded from what is actually the case to what might be the case. One appreciates that expansion best, obviously, when the realization of the might-be involves one's own activity. I will not spell out the expansion here,[6] but in the following chapter, I give a single illustration of the movement to decision.

Even this skimpy treatment should enable you to appreciate vaguely the recurrence of the basic three levels within this new context. That new context is the context of human doing, of will, and willingness. It is from that experienced context that the word "good" gets its descriptive meaning. But one moves to an explanatory understanding of *good* only to the degree to which self-attention to will has been successfully attempted. That successful attempt would reveal that there is a certain duality in the meaning of *good* corresponding to the two orientations of will, the orientation of complacency or serenity and the orientation of concern. That meaning involves two related sets of terms and relations. A parallel may help here. Just as insight into the diagram of a circle yields the definition of a circle which involves the concepts of line, point, etc., so insight into the experiences of will yields such related terms. In the orientation of complacency these terms are basically the mutually defining *good* and *complacency*; in the concern orientation the basic terms are *concern, end, good, value*. Beyond this indication I do not wish to go.[7] The expert will recognize here a focal source for the duality of St. Thomas's treatment of the good. The initiate will acknowledge the parallel between the scientific self-attention treatment of the will and the scientific in other fields. As I remarked, the terms "complacency" and "concern" are technical or scientific in the accepted sense of those words. Insofar as the methodological education of a person is successful, familiarity with such words will not lead to contempt for their scientific meaning and its relevance, or to a loss of the sense of mystery.

Our basic three levels may be appreciated in terms of the good, either as an object of complacency or as an object of concern. Consider an order of affairs, for example, a five-year economic plan which has been decided on and is going into operation. You will appreciate that this is a third-level phenomenon. That level involves the realization of an order—economic, social, etc.—that was considered to be good. That order or plan was perhaps one of several that arose from an understanding of the concrete situation and its possibilities: it was an answer to a What-question. Now you can appreciate without much difficulty that the answer to such a What-question is complex, something more than butter and beef. It is not just a collection or a listing of particular goods. Each of us has the experience of the need of such goods, be it through hunger or thirst or, on a higher level, through the desire to understand. But the possible dynamic social structure is not any basket of goods, but an ordering of goods—it is a good of order. It is, of course, at such a good of order that a party or government policy should aim, not yielding to the temptation either to promise particular goods or to promote some abstract ideal. But since the mass of people lean spontaneously toward the palpable, a policy of campaigning if not of government profitably leans similarly toward what appeals to the eye and the appetite rather than to the ordering mind. Here we touch on the large topic of bias,[8] but I pass over it in favor of a words on the related question of individual genuineness, close as it is to the orientation of this introductory book.

I may assume that most of the readers of this book are interested in genuineness on the level of intellectual development. That interest is the interest of a person, not of a pure intelligence, and so it is multiply conditioned in its concrete pursuit. The focal element in that interest is the drive of wonder native to all men, but that focal element is meshed with degrees of willingness and the complexity of the psyche. I have said nothing so far about the psychic dimensions of human development; I have said little, indeed, about development at all. Yet I may appeal to the reader's general familiarity with human development to assert that genuineness is linked with sustained human development, and that the focus of that development lies in intelligence. Implicitly, the discussion of metaethics lays stress on the central role of intelligence in human doing, on the spontaneous demand within the person for consistency between his knowing and his doing. That stress is related to an opposite tendency which would leave a chasm between knowledge and love, or between truth and ethical imperatives. It would, too, undercut the apparent ultimacy of such categories as egoism and altruism. It is intelligence and reasonableness that assume the ultimate position. Intelligence reveals to man *a* real order of things which places himself and his neighbor on a par within that order. It is to intelligence he must look if he seeks the development of that order. My reader understands all this, to some extent.

But to what extent? And here I return to the basic point of this book. If I say that it is to intelligence that we must look for personal and contemporary development, I mean it not in any normal or descriptive sense but in the sense emergent from the metempirical inquiry which I seek to indicate. To ask for intelligence in behavior is nothing strange in many civilizations: *sois sage!* More properly, one may specify the general norms of human behavior in terms relating to our four levels: be attentive, be intelligent, be reasonable, be responsible, terms which everyone understands. But the manner in which everyone may understand such terms and norms is the common-sense manner. The manner in which I assert the need for a turn to intelligence, the need for a new manner of intelligence, is the manner of the horizon of interiority indicated in chapter one. So, in these past chapters we have had an initial engagement with the metaquestion, What is it to be attentive, intelligent, reasonable, responsible?

Talcott Parsons and Neil Smelser indicate, among the barriers to the development of socio-economics, that which comes from the sociological tradition: "A major isolating factor has been a revolt, perhaps, against the subtle ways in which the ideology of economic thinking has permeated the wider intellectual atmosphere."[9] Our concern here is with a deeper and still more subtle ideology which permeates both economic and sociological thinking. Looking back to the conclusion of chapter five and forward to the conclusion of chapter seven I might say that the persons who exchange goods and views, pledges and presents, are not such obvious objects of inquiry as many sociologists and economists think. Could it be that the core of the phenomena of interpersonal relations is almost systematically excluded from serious scientific interest and investigation by the conventions of contemporary inquiry?

But, while I raise these broader issues of the Great Ascent, I do so only with a reminder that, in the present introductory inquiry, the phenomenon is you.

Notes

[1] See F. E. Crowe, S.J., "Complacency and Concern in the Writings of St. Thomas," *Theological Studies* (20), 1959.

[2] F. E. Crowe, *op. cit.*, 363–382.

[3] The diagram itself suggests the complexity resulting from the meshing of willing and sensibility, but I omit the consideration of this from our introductory reflections.

[4] *Summa Theologica*, Pars Prima, q. 87, a. 4.

[5] "St. Thomas and the Concrete Operabile," *Sciences Ecclesiastiques*, 1955–56; "Complacency and Concern in the Writings of St. Thomas," *Theological Studies* (20), 1959.

[6] See B. Lonergan, *Insight*, 612–6; CWL 3, 636–39.

[7] See endnote 4 of chapter 2 above.

[8] B. Lonergan, *Insight*, 191–206 and 218–42; CWL 3, 214–231 and 244–267.

[9] T. Parsons and N. Smelser, *Economy and Society, A Study in the Integration of Economic and Social Theory*, New York, Free Press, 1969, xviii.

Chapter 7 ~ The Economy of Truth

B ehind all the symbols, however, rests the central requirement of
faith. Money serves its indispensable purposes as long as we believe
in it. It ceases to the moment we do not. Money has well been called the
promise men live by.[1]

The collaboration which constitutes an economy is a collaboration of believers.
A very elementary step, then, in investigating presuppositions of economics is
the analysis of oneself as believer. Here I would like to initiate your reflections
on yourself as believer by teasing out somewhat popularly elements of the
process.

Most people, perhaps, listen to the weather forecast on radio or television
merely because, like the advertisements, it is interjected between other items. It
is listened to with varying degrees of attention and of skepticism. Some scarcely
attend to it at all; others are fascinated by a mumbo jumbo about pressure and
depressions; still others are sufficiently informed to follow the bulletin
intelligently. The skepticism of some extends to considering the reverse of the
forecast as nearer the truth; not a few regard it as little more reliable than putting
a wet finger in the air or noting the color of the evening sky; and there are those
who concede that the morrow's weather will probably follow the pattern
indicated. Now while all the elements and attitudes in the above description of
a belief situation are of interest and grist for self-attention, our present concern
is with the main lines of the meaning of the sharing of truth.

Obviously, any listener and the weatherman are in different positions with
regard to knowledge of the morrow's weather. Let us suppose for the moment
that the weatherman who made out the report had at his disposal all the
required instruments and that he made the observations and calculations
himself. That being the case, in coming to his conclusions about the future
weather he depended only on his own experience and observations and on his
own scientific knowledge. He himself considered all the relevant factors,
weighed the evidence and intelligently arrived at the present forecast. Coming
thus to an intelligent conclusion includes appreciating just how certain the
conclusion is. So, the weatherman appreciates that he is not infallible, that the
forecast enjoys a degree of probability, that its fulfillment depends on various
complex conditions. Consider now the man who listens intelligently to the

forecast and reasonably accepts it. No more than the weatherman does he take it to be infallible: Accepting it intelligently he accepts it with a degree of certainty similar to the certainty of the weatherman, for he accepts both the scientific effort and its limitations. Ultimately, then, the weatherman and the listener are informed about tomorrow's weather and the listener are informed about tomorrow's weather, yet differently so. I will denote that difference here by saying that whereas the weatherman knows, the listener in question believes.[2] But let this not seem a predetermining of the issue by a choice of the word "belief." The present chapter is not a prolonged dictionary definition. I am not listing the uses of the word "belief." I am trying to generate some understanding of the experience which we usually call believing. I take the listener's acceptance of the weather forecast as an instance of that experience. Some may object that this does not square with their notion of belief: Let me bypass this objection conveniently by saying that although we could label the experience with some other word, we opt for this word already in use for a variety of similar human experiences. That much being clear we may return to our task.

I say that what the weatherman knows, the listener believes. Furthermore, I will keep rigidly to this terminology. I will use the word "know" only when the knower peruses the relevant data, rightly understands what must be understood in the particular case, and intelligently arrives at true judgment. When this is not the case, as with the listener, I use the word "believe." By way of illustration let me note that many of my readers may not know that Ireland is an island, but I take it that you believe it is! Again, for most of us the circulation of the blood is a matter of belief. Briefly, whereas knowledge is immanently generated, belief is the acceptance of reliably communicated knowledge.

Before going on to analyze the experience I have called belief, let us face a more general question: Why is there such a thing as belief? Clearly, belief can be said to meet a real need. So, one may listen to the weather forecast precisely because the activities of the morrow are to be determined by it. One needs information about the coming weather in order to act and since personal investigation is out of the question, one is willing to rely on the experience, understanding, and judgment of others for this information. More generally, belief is part of all successful human collaboration, and collaboration is essential to human progress. Consider, for example, the ordinary occurrences during work on a building site. The crane operator does not know that the load is ready for lifting: he relies on the knowledge of the man who signals him. The bricklayer raises no questions about the stress and strain in the walls. More remotely, the engineer does not check the logarithm tables or slide rule at his disposal. And so on. Without this collaboration which in every link includes belief, work on a building site would be a riot of individualism, fragmented into eccentric investigations into elementary problems, and the labor could scarcely be expected to yield us much more than a complex of stone igloos. And clearly what holds for a building holds much more for the building of an economy.

The need for belief, however, goes deeper than the requirements of immediate action and successful cooperation. The continued labors of scientists bear witness to the unlimited desire of man for knowledge. Now no one man can know everything about everything. Further, no man can afford to begin at the beginning, nor can he investigate all he presupposes, nor indeed can he alone adequately verify the theories he may evolve. Basic to the methodology of advancing science, and so obvious as not to be adverted to, is that no man confines his assets to his personal experience, understanding, and judgment. The advance of human science is a matter of a collaboration which extends from nation to nation, from generation to generation. And the only alternative to that collaboration is a primitive ignorance. The collaboration, and the belief which it involves, even if not acknowledged in so many words, nonetheless exist and multiply continually. No mathematician nowadays masters all the branches of his trade; experimental scientists rely on the reports of colleagues, of predecessors, and of the mathematicians; economists do not normally take time out to check published statistics. No doubt it is a fact that any of these men might settle down to understand and check personally what their work presupposes. Yet it is no less a fact that they do not do this. Besides, such a successful check is practically impossible. Human science is so basically a collective business that no scientist can have immanently generated knowledge of the really significant evidence, for the significant evidence for any theory is precisely the common testimony of scientists, past and present, regarding the verification of the theory in their respective investigations.

Returning to our initial weather-forecasting example, we find that both the needs mentioned, the need to do and the more fundamental need to know, are illustrated by it. For besides the need for information about the morrow's weather on the part of the particular listener, there is, it is hoped, the scientific satisfaction of the weatherman in adequately forecasting. Of course, the supposition that the weatherman knows—quite apart from the puzzle regarding the impossibility of knowledge of the future—is only for argument's sake. Even if only one station were necessary and all the instruments were to hand, the weatherman does not *know* that the instruments are reliable.

I have been spelling this point out because contrary to a common view that science is knowledge, science or any other part of our stock of truth is largely belief, and if you check through some of your own possession of truth you will find your knowledge inextricably meshed with a far larger proportion of belief. Both knowledge and belief are ways of coming to and possessing truth. In the first case one is relying on one's own understanding and experience; in the second case one is relying on the understanding and experience of another. The second way of coming to and possessing the truth is basically possible because of the first. For when you reach knowledge or truth, it is not just truth for you, a subjective truth. The truth you reach is independent of you, and that independence makes it detachable, communicable. We are here extending the efforts of chapters four and five, and it is as well now to pause and recall that context. You may well, especially on a first reading, have come this far in this present chapter without, so to speak, bringing with you that context. It reads extremely easily; its offer of a distinction between the two experiences, named knowing and believing, is not startling; and one should not take long to digest the suggestion that more than ninety per cent of one's store of truth is belief. So, as I say, it is as well to pause and take stock of the horizons of writing and reading.

We are trying to initiate dialogue within the horizon of interiority, and it takes no small psychic effort to take up an adequate stance:

> No man is born in that pattern; no one reaches it easily; no one remains in it permanently; and when some other pattern is dominant, then the self of our self-affirmation seems quite different from one's actual self, the universe of being seems as unreal as Plato's noetic heaven, and objectivity spontaneously becomes a matter of meeting persons and dealing with things that are really out there.[3]

The trouble with initial descriptive classification is that its language at present is that of common sense, and without the effort to contextualize it with the mood of chapter five further moves into interiority may be blocked by the control-potential of common sense language and by "a demand for a metaphysics that is grounded, not in the impalpable potentiality of explanation, but in the manifest truth of description."[4] The early chapters initiated a move toward knowledge of knowledge. Our present effort is toward a knowledge of belief, but my contribution in this short work can only be a rather broad phenomenology. In the light of the epilogue the reader may be able to glimpse the complexity of an adequate heuristic of a belief situation.

A parallel from another area of methodology may help. Paul Weiss prefaces his lengthy effort to specify development with the remark on the apparent triviality of the question, What is development? "Does not everybody have some notion of what development implies? Undoubtedly most of us have. But when it comes to formulating these notions they usually turn out to be vague." [5] Similarly what belief is may seem initially evident. But a self-questioning effort at formulation will reveal that while specimens 'o belief are abundant in our daily exchange, that asset in the economy of truth is far from an explained asset.

We may now proceed, in a better context, with some large pieces of the puzzle, What do I do when I believe?

First of all, coming to believe a given truth involves a complex of personal judgments prior to the particular act of belief. They may be prior as a habitual pattern of thinking and living. This type of prior judgment we have already touched on when we considered the role of belief in human living: Whether we admit it or not, we already act on the conviction that belief in general is of value, that it is of value both to communicate to others the truths one has reached and to accept from others the truths they have reached. But besides this background of judgments on belief in general, there is in the case of any given proposition a more particular set of preliminary judgments concerning the accuracy of the communication from the original source of the truth and the reliability of the source itself. It is evident from our discussion of truth that there is such a source: If there is a particular proposition which is proposed as true, that proposition cannot be belief for everyone, since belief is a secondary way of possessing truth. The particular proposition must be, not belief, but knowledge for someone.

Now one might well reach the preliminary judgments on the reliability of the source by seeking out that source. But it is well to note that even if one is fortunate enough to have a personal interview with the original knower, one is looking for evidence, not for the particular proposition, but for belief. Thus, one might interview a mathematician in order to see what sort of creature he is as a preliminary to believing his tables of logarithms. But to ask him to provide evidence that the logarithm of one is zero is another matter, for one would then be seeking knowledge, not grounds for belief. This example merely serves to stress that the preliminary judgments are concerned with the evidence for belief in a particular truth, not with the evidence for the truth. For reaching these preliminary judgments there can be no general rule. One moves as best one can within the four-fold norm of the previous chapter. So one may rely on personal knowledge of another's character. One may advert to motives, to ability, to opportunity to deceive, to the check of scientific progress, to the exposing power of historical research, and so on. In this way one moves from a basic conviction that, in general, belief is a human good to a judgment on the good of this particular belief. More accurately, the preliminary judgments lead one to grasp as unconditioned the value of deciding to believe this particular proposition, and this grasp finds its expression in a corresponding judgment of value. This judgment of value calls for a comment. The value in question is precisely the value of the personal possession of the particular truth. If this notion of value is to take on meaning for the reader, he or she must advert to truths in personal experience which have such a quality. No doubt it is of value to the engineer to accept the table of logarithms if he is to get on with his job. No doubt it is of value to the theoretical physicist to accept the experimentalist's results regarding neutrinos. No doubt many people consider it of value to accept telephone and television communications as true. Still, none of these examples may hit it off for you. Even if you do accept as true the broad lines of news reports, the effort to isolate the preliminary judgments of value in this case may be too much for you. So it is up to you to seek out and exploit—with an energy paralleling and transcending the sophisticated efforts of phenomenologists—occurrences of personal believing that lend themselves to self-digestion.

The preliminary judgments, then, lead to a certain appreciation of the worth of a particular belief, and this appreciation finds its expression in a judgment of the value of deciding to believe the particular proposition. From this appreciation, or intelligent grasp, the judgment necessarily follows, and if, in fact, we make this judgment then we cannot both be reasonable and fail to decide to believe. And from that decision there follows naturally the act of belief. There is, one might say, a clear follow-through from grasp of value to belief: to draw out the metaphor, at the bottom of the swing occurs the judgment of value, the swing naturally continues to a reasonable responsible belief, yet the whole movement depends on the downswing which ends in a grasp of the value of deciding to believe. This grasp of the sufficiency of the evidence for the judgment of value is clearly the key act in the process. The preliminary judgments lead to it; the sequence of other acts follow from it. That grasp is had insofar as one intelligently appreciates the general value of belief, the particular relevance of the given proposition, the accuracy of the communication for the source, and reliability of the source. It is not a matter of listing premises, of deducing conclusions or constructing syllogisms. No doubt these may help toward it. But there is no alternative to intelligent and critical reflection on the sufficiency of the accumulated evidence for the belief. Finally, as indicated earlier, human certainty is a human thing which admits of a spectrum of degrees falling below absolute certainty.

While I distinguish the judgment, the decision, and the assent of the act of belief, these three form a tight sequence following the basic grasp of value. Consider first the judgment of value. It resembles any other judgment that we make, for all reasonable judgments follow from an intelligent grasp of the evidence for them. So, for example, the oculist does not judge that a person needs glasses without testing his eyes and appreciating the sufficiency of these tests. Like any other judgment, too, the judgment of value can be false if the preliminary investigation is inadequate or biased or influenced adversely by other desires. It differs, however, from ordinary and theoretical judgments of fact in that it is a judgment, one may say, of possible fact, of value, and the particular value in question is the good of possessing a particular truth.

The decision that follows the judgment of value, like any other decision, is free and responsible. Like any other decision it is reasonable and good if the prior judgment is honest, favorable, and correct. Like any other decision, it depends on the intelligent grasp of a possible course of action. But the course of action envisaged in taking this particular decision is not an external activity, but the internal act of assent to the particular proposition.

Lastly, there is the crowning act of believing. By it the particular truth in question is accepted as true. The act by which you accept that truth is similar to any other act of judgment, for in any act of judgment one affirms or denies a certain proposition of to be true with the simple Yes or No of reason. However, while in a judgment which is knowledge, what moves us to it is our own grasp of the evidence for it, in a judgment which is an act of belief we are moved also by the decision to take advantage of a particular human collaboration in the pursuit of truth. Such is the economy of human truth: what is scarce in knowledge can be abundant in belief.

Much more might be added on the present topic, indications of the self-attentive investigation of the area of mistaken beliefs, doubts, neural and affective conditioning and such like. But these topics would carry us beyond the introductory level. This is not to say, however, that they are not central data for metaeconomic or metasocio-economic inquiry. Paul Samuelson remarked once,

> If I depart from the narrow field of economics, I must confess that the writings of sociologists like Parsons seem to me to be seriously empty because they never seem even to ask the question of what difference it makes to have social action part of a maximizing value system.[6]

May I parallel Samuelson's remark by drawing attention to the altogether more serious neglect, both by sociologists and economists, of the possibility of an explanatory interiority-meaning for such terms as "belief," "propensity," "decision-making," "choice," "investment," "contract," "action"? Galileo's patience with the possibilities of an inclined plane transformed a descriptive and mythic physics of motion into the beginnings of an explanatory science. Perhaps self-attentive methodology could benefit the human sciences as measurement (itself, of course, a complex human action!) benefited physics? At all events, if money is "the promise men live by," surely there is something obscurantist in not raising the question self-attentive science, What, then, is a promise?

Notes

[1] R. L. Heilbroner, *The Economic Problem*, New Jersey, Prentice-Hall, 1972, 352.

[2] The acute reader will notice a flaw here, which like the flaw in my definition of the ellipse in chapter three may lead to further insight. Knowledge of the future is impossible for either man or God. Further insights are required to make the facts of future-oriented faith intelligible.

[3] B. Lonergan, *Insight*, 385; CWL 3, 411.

[4] Ibid., 505; CWL 3, 529.

[5] P. Weiss, *Principles of Development*, New York, Holt, 1939, 1. See also endnote 8 of my chapter 10.

[6] P. A. Samuelson, "Maximum Principles in Analytic Economics," *The American Economic Review*, LXII (1972), 258.

Chapter 8 ~ Technico-Aesthetic
Objectifications of Self-Assets

Afamiliarity with the elements of logic can be obtained by a very modest effort in a very short time. Until one has made notable progress in cognitional analysis, one is constantly tempted to mistake the rules of logic for the laws of thought.[1]

The reader will notice an echo here of our discussion of the square-root rule. Indeed from that particular illustration one might gain insight into the same problem as it occurs right through the daily life of technological man. A bus or an economy can with some success be guided without an understanding of the dynamics of the interlocking parts. But what of breakdowns or of parts that are miscast—especially if the parts be persons?

I would hope that the reader would eventually pursue such reflections. But my interest here is narrower. I wish to give indications of how self-attentive methodology opens up the possibility of a radical renovation of logic, mathematics and their foundations. [2] The discussion and the possible renovation are, however, paradigmatic.

Let me begin with a simple geometrical illustration. I recall again that our interest is methodological: the need, therefore, is for the reader to attend to himself or herself as well as to the geometry. A first thing to note, of course, is that while the puzzle is printed the reader will very spontaneously—I hope—reach for pen and paper and draw a diagram. Obviously this fits into the general theorem regarding the need for phantasms in order to understand. But now I wish to note the further point that some phantasms are better than others. This point will carry us much further than might be suspected at this stage. I may hint at this here by noting that as well as the seen logical symbol there is the affect-laden sight of a city. More remotely there is the possibility, indicated by the titles of this and the following chapter, of an axial transformation of the world of arts and crafts. But if that possibility is to become a probability it will be only through detailed self-attention such as we are here engaging in. Let us proceed then with our illustration.

In geometry it is quite clear that the written-out problem and even the written-out solution can be far less adequate than a suitable diagram from which, one might say, the solution stares one in the face. The solution written out is a symbolic expression of our understanding—we use the word "symbol" in the mathematical sense, as an equivalent to sign, and not in the sense of affect-laden image. The print is a series of conventional signs of meaning, and it is at a remove from what is to be understood. At the other extreme there are such images as the drawn circle: when one is searching for the definition of a circle it is the roundness of the drawn circle that one concentrates on. Wonder is directly engaged with the object to be understood. Trying to understand the properties of parallel lines provides an illustration of a somewhat different type of image. One cannot draw or imagine indefinitely produced straight lines. In this instance one may say that the image is virtual, and the key to the use of such an image is the mediation or intervention of understanding: the lines are drawn a bit but thought of as indefinitely produced. Understanding can dominate the image even further, as with conventional language. We settle just what a given image is to stand for through the intervention of definition. So it is with the conventional meaning of the sight and sound and braille of the English language. But before we say more about this settling of meaning and the judicious choice of image let us expose our puzzle in the conventional symbolism of print.

In a circle of, say, unit radius, two diameters, perpendicular to each other, are drawn. From an arbitrary point P on the circumference two perpendiculars PR and PS are drawn to the two diameters. The problem is, What is the ratio of RS to the radius? You have now drawn the figure? Perhaps even easily solved the puzzle? Your reaction to the puzzle and your solution of it will depend very much on your habits of mathematics. If mathematics leaves you cold, then you may find it hard enough to make a proper diagram much less solve the puzzle. If you are a mathematician, then the solution is just too obvious. If you fall in between these two extremes then you may draw and mark and puzzle, even try trigonometry. Joining R and S will be an evident thing to do; but it may take a pedagogue to adequately dispose the phantasm by the drawing of another line. The line to draw is the line joining the center to the point P, say OP. Eureka! With the insight emerges the solution, the relation between RS and the radius.

Now note that the solution can be formulated or thrown into syllogistic form, and this will help you get some light on features of the syllogism which are often misrepresented. We have, therefore, the syllogism:

$$RS = OP$$
$$\text{and } OP = \text{Radius};$$
$$\text{therefore } RS = \text{Radius}.$$

In this light I may note important characteristics of procedure. We started, not with two premises, but with the conclusion in the form:

$$RS \ ? \ \text{Radius}$$

Our search, through diagram, was for a middle term, and the middle term was supplied as soon as one adverted to the significance of OP. Only then can the syllogism be constructed. To coin an expression for this constructing, one might say that the insight is crystallized into a syllogism. This does not mean, of course, that somehow the insight has been pinned down on a page. What has happened is that we have given the insight explicit symbolic expression. Giving all the relevant insights explicit symbolic expression is by no means always an easy thing to do, even when it can be done. Modern geometers have found fault with Euclid in this matter. There are insights involved in the *Elements* which are not explicitly acknowledged either in the axioms or in the theorems, yet which were not uncrystallizable. We may illustrate this neatly from a piece of Felix Klein's discussion of geometry.[3] We need not enter into the details of this problem. Roughly, it concerns (cf. p. 88) drawing a line from 1' to ½, across a triangle yOx. In the process he remarks that

> the unique constructibility . . . of the point ½ as the intersection of the x axis with the path curve from 1' . . . would be assured if we only knew that this path curve really cut the x axis. Of course, no one would doubt that, intuitively, but in the framework of our axiomatic deduction we need a special axiom, the so-called betweenness axiom for the plane. This axiom states that if a line enters a triangle through a side, it must leave it through another side—a trivial fact of our space perception which requires emphasis as such, because it is independent of the other axioms.[4]
>
> . . .
>
> If we omit this, as Euclid does, we cannot reach the ideal of *a* pure logical control of geometry. We must continually recur to the figure.[5]

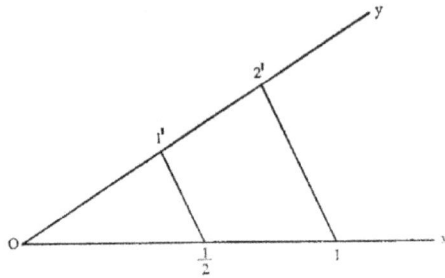

Let me note further that our simple puzzle and solution is *a* paradigm of how Euclid and company may well have proceeded in most of the Euclidean theorems. They did not proceed step by step down the page of the modern textbook, from the stated theorem, to the fully constructed diagram, to the step by step deduction beneath. One should note, too, the significance of this for the teaching of geometry. Too often the pupils begin, not with the thrill of a puzzle but with the top of the page, and at most they get a vague line-by-line comprehension of the theorem. Memory is burdened, and examinations consist in filling out theorems—from the bottom and top of the page!—and passing over the riders.

We may return now to a brief consideration of the simple symbolic expression of understanding which is the syllogism. Let us distinguish here just two main types of syllogism and with them associate the two main types of proof. These two main types are related to the two main types of question discussed earlier.

Consider first the syllogism which is associated with the What-question. The syllogism given in connection with our simple problem was of this type, and it may be called the syllogism helping toward direct understanding. Now "helping toward understanding" is precisely the role that this syllogism can play. This "helping toward understanding" is related to what was mentioned earlier about the judicious choice of symbolism. The syllogism is so structured as to facilitate the understanding of the relevant relation. Much more, of course, could be said about the syllogism, but I wish to emphasize this one point: that the syllogism is not a mysterious replacement for understanding. Again, one may look on the syllogism as a proof of the conclusion, but this can only mean that the structure facilitates a grasp of the implication of the conclusion in the premises. One might note, too, that such structures facilitate the checking, the Is-question, relating to that grasp: this could lead to a discussion of the question, among others, of consistency in wider areas, a larger study. At all events it should be evident to the reader that one definite type of proof is exemplified here, one which occurs centrally on the level of the What-question. It is deductive proof, the proof normally associated with mathematics.

Besides deductive proof there is proof in the sense of verification. In this sense one can prove that the law of gravity holds, or that iron does not float on water. This sort of proof is centrally associated with the Is-question, and it is reached by a reflective act of understanding which grasps sufficiency of evidence. Just as in the case of direct understanding, so here one can be helped to reach that grasp by syllogistic expression. I have, indeed, made use of such expression in chapter four, but there it fulfilled the more subtle function of helping the reader to grasp the grasp, so to speak.

> As has been seen already, the function of syllogistic expression is not to eliminate but to facilitate the occurrence of the reflective act of understanding. A parrot or an electronic computer can send forth signs in a syllogistic pattern; but neither can grasp the virtually unconditioned; and neither can be subjected to the rational necessity that results in a judgment.[6]

One can lay out the evidence, the case, symbolically, showing the links in such a way as to make it easy for a person to move to a grasp of the sufficiency of the evidence and the fulfillment of the conditions. But it is quite another thing for that person to grasp, or indeed to be willing to try to grasp. The horse may be brought to the water.

I leave to the reader the task of manufacturing syllogisms which are related to the Is-question. I would like to note, however, that the process of coming to belief can also be helped in the same way. Consider for example the syllogism:

Whatever A tells me is credible, and to be believed by me,
A tells me X;
Therefore X is credible and to be believed by me.

As in all syllogisms of this type, the "therefore" in the conclusion represents the possibility of a reflective act of understanding. As the previous chapter indicated, the transition to the act of belief is not just a matter of reflective understanding: will and willingness are involved. But the same basic principle holds of "suitable lay-out" of evidence, steps, links.

Let us go a little further into this question of suitable lay-out, judicious choice of signs, etc. It is a region of concern for pedagogues and advertisers, but our interest here, let us not forget, is a metainterest. What is the significance of symbolism? First, symbolism is, in a certain sense, a "lay-out," an objectification of mind. We have gone far enough now in cognitional analysis, perhaps, to appreciate that this does not mean that understanding has been pressed into a page, that truth has been made so independent of a particular mind that it exists without any mind. The objectification in question here is closely related to the suitability of the lay-out. Consider again the illustration in chapter three of the taking of a square root. There we noted that there was a technique by which the square root of a number could be arrived at. Any schoolboy would do it with a little practice, yet without understanding the Why of it all. The symbolism is suitable, the technique far from subtle. Try on the other hand getting the square root of the same number expressed in Roman numerals. Again, even if one understands the Why of the technique, still one takes the root without any effort of understanding, as something routine. Nor are logic and mathematics isolated instances of such procedure, of in-built implication and routine movement to result. You may think of the watchmaker with precise skill but perhaps no understanding of the Why of the watch, of balance-wheel, and escapement, or you may consider the enormous development of modern technology. An interesting instance of coupling modern technology with adequate logical symbolism is provided by the computerizing of the famous *Principia Mathematica* of Whitehead and Russell:

> The author is interested in proving theorems with computing machines. In this connection he wrote three programmes for an IBM 704. The first programme provides a decision procedure for the propositional calculus which leads the machine to print out a proof or disproof according as the given proposition is a theorem or not. It was found that all theorems of the first five chapters of the *Principia Mathematica* were proved in 37 minutes, 12/13 of the time being used for read-ins and printouts. The second programme instructs the machine to form propositions of the propositional calculus and select non-trivial theorems. The author writes that the results were disappointing in so far as too few theorems were excluded as being trivial. The third programme is for the predicate calculus with equality. It is claimed that this programme can find and print out proofs for about 85% of the theorems in Chapters 5–10 of *P.M.* in about an hour.[7]

We may now turn back to consider the developments of modern symbolic logic. In the light of the present discussion, one should be in a better position to appreciate what is going on in this field.

One might consider mathematical logic as a study of deductive systems, a study which generates a series of hypotheses on the nature of deductive systems. Now, as any logician will tell you, such a study would scarcely be possible without the elaboration of a large set of symbols with definite rules of construction for complete expressions. In other words, the modern understanding of deduction depends on what is, equivalent to a technological development on the level of sign. But one must be careful here to distinguish between the symbolism and the object of understanding. Consider, for example, the effort we made in chapter three to reach a definition of the ellipse. In reaching that definition we were helped by the diagram, the operations and such symbols as AP + BP. Generally in analytic geometry one "leans on" both diagrams and symbolism, and anyone who has actually done analytic geometry will appreciate the value of the symbolism in the solution of problems, how at times it, as it were, takes over. At any rate, the object understood in that example was the ellipse, and what we reached was the definition of the ellipse—which, we recall, is unimaginable. The reader may notice a certain amount of ambiguity in the previous sentence. There are indeed two objects understood, but differently so, and it is helpful to introduce a suggestive technical distinction. We may speak of the imagined ellipse, as the "moving object" for intelligence, and of the definition of the ellipse as the "terminal object." Through this illustration it is perhaps easier to appreciate the statement that mathematical logic has as terminal object the definition of deductive system, this being understood in its broadest sense, involving thus the range of inverse-insight theorems, like those discussed by J. Ladrière,[8] and n-valued logics. Here again I skip over interesting points of discussion such as the factual reference of such systems and the question of truth in logic. I stick rather to the central point of the chapter: the role of symbols in the control and generation of insight. Just as in analytic geometry, the symbolism in logic can carry one on, suggest changes, expose inadequacies. The expression of axiom systems in apt symbolism, for example, may be called virtual images: recall the similar cases of parallel lines and distinguish between the two types of virtuality.[9]

Again, the same symbolic technique can play the role of "moving object" in a series of different fields, "isomorphic fields" as they are called. Here I may be losing the general reader, but the mathematician may recall such illustrations as lattice theory, or the associated power of implicit definition. Stefan Banach, in a paper which developed the basic notions of Banach spaces, put the matter well: "This present work has the object of establishing certain theorems that hold in several different branches of mathematics, which will be specified later. However, in order to avoid proving these theorems for each branch individually, which would be very wearisome, I have chosen a different way, which is this: I consider in a general way sets of elements for which I postulate certain properties. From these I deduce theorems and then I prove for each separate branch of mathematics that the postulates adopted are true."[10]

I have stressed here the relation between the possibility of the investigation of the fields of logical relations and the development of suitable symbolic techniques. I mentioned, in passing, the region which deals with limitation theorems, a region which marks one type of limitation on a symbolic expression. Thus, according to Church's thesis, "recursive undecidibility is equivalent to effective undecidibility, i.e., nonexistence of a mechanical decision procedure for theoremhood. The nonexistence of such a mechanical procedure means that ingenuity is required for determining whether any given well-formed formula is a theorem."[11] Various other limitations of symbolic expression are noted by Lonergan in his discussion of the limitations of the treatise.[12] Here I am concentrating on limitations on the level of mathematics and logic. I note further that even in the strict derivation of conclusions of modern deductive systems, with fully formulated axioms and rules of inference, what Mendelson calls "ingenuity" and Suppes calls "intuition" or "insight" is necessary. To quote an example from Suppes, ". . . to derive from the axioms what is known as the *right-hand cancellation law* . . . the crucial step is realizing what substitution in axiom (1) is appropriate. . . . For with this insight goes the perception that $zoz^1 = e$ by virtue of axiom (3)."[13]

There are, then, the casual insights which, as it were, step through the net of formulation. It is the business of formal logic, of course, to trap all that can be trapped: "Its function is to make explicit all the essential elements whether they are obvious or not."[14] That quotation serves to recall Lonergan's significant work, in the article cited, on the reduction to one general form of all valid forms of inference. Needless to say, to appreciate his discussion and conclusion you must be operating in the self-attentive mode. Otherwise, you will be constantly puzzled about what he is at, you will wonder what all the fuss is about, and you "may miss the turning leading to an understanding of understanding."[15] It is no easy matter to self-attend one's way understandingly through the article cited.

In this context one may note the discussion of W. Kneale and M. Kneale of Aristotle's neglect of the form of inference.[16] This neglect leads to an exaggeration of the opposition of the Aristotelian position and modem logic, the axiom systems of which so evidently involve formalization of the properties of inference.[17] Obviously there are other reasons for the opposition of Aristotelian and Scholastic logic to modern logic, but we note only this one, and the relevance of Lonergan's reduction to its removal. The problem is to reach an understanding of the roots of reasoning. We are not God, nor are we angels. Our understanding develops: reasoning is motion toward understanding, a Motion involving the symbol. The simple hypothetical argument expresses the general form of that motion: "Just as 'so that' and 'in order that' express the relations of efficient and final causality, so also 'because,' although' and 'if' are the special tools of the reasoning man,"[18] and that motion "comes to a term in the intuitive apprehension of a field of implications, interrelations."[19]

A little Latin declension brings us from *inferre* to the illative sense of Newman, and a hint to the reader that the form of deductive inference which Lonergan uses in *Insight*[20] has a history and a significance that are far from evident at first sight. In this region of the Is-question we find, too, a further instance of the limitation of symbolisms.[21]

Some indication has been given of the enrichment of foundational work in logic and mathematics. In an introductory book that is as much as can be attempted. I have tried nonetheless to give occasional glimpses beyond that level, and one might expect that an axial transformation of volumes of symbols such as the *Journal of Symbolic Logic* would be quite a shift in the objectification of understanding which they are. An aspect of that shift would be a linguistic or symbolic feedback far beyond the eccentric Gödelian formulae "talking about themselves." As Lonergan remarks, "At a higher level of linguistic development, the possibility of insight is achieved by a linguistic feedback, by expressing the subjective experience in words and as subjective."[22] But with that hint of radical change I move on to consider artistic objectification and feedback. My considerations there must remain under the same restriction. One must push for some meta-understanding of the artistry that is familiar prior to pushing for some heuristic glimpse of axial art.

Notes

[1] B. Lonergan, *Insight*, 573; CWL 3, 596.

[2] P. McShane, "The Foundations of Mathematics," *Modern Schoolman* (40) 1963, 373-87.

[3] F. Klein, *Geometry*, New York, Dover, 1956, 165.

[4] Ibid., 165.

[5] Ibid., 201.

[6] B. Lonergan, *Insight*, 710; CWL 3, 732.

[7] Steven Orey, in a review of Hao Wang's work reported in *IBM Journal of Research and Development* (4) 1960, 2-22; *Journal of Symbolic Logic* (30) 1965, 249.

[8] Jean Ladrière, *Les Limitations Internes des Formalismes*, Paris, Gauthier-Villars, 1957.

[9] One could be led further here by reflecting on the problem of defining a geometry: cf. my *Randomness, Statistics and Emergence*, Gill Macmillan and Notre Dame, 1970, 114 ff.; Axial Publishing, 2021, 95–100.

[10] "Sur les operations dans les ensembles abstraits et leur application aux equations integrals," *Fundamenta Mathematica* (3) 1922, 134. The translation is by W. Sawyer in his *A Path to Modern Mathematics*, Penguin, 193. I may remark here on the significance of Sawyer's books as laying implicit stress on insight into phantasm. As well as his series of Pelican books, note his paperback *A Concrete Approach to Abstract Algebra*, San Francisco, 1959.

[11] E. Mendelson, *Introduction to Mathematical Logic*, Princeton, Van Nostrand, 1964, 151.

[12] B. Lonergan, *Insight*, 573–7; 595–600.

[13] P. Suppes, *Introduction to Logic*, Princeton, Van Nostrand, 1957, 106.

[14] B. Lonergan, "The Form of Inference," *Collection*, 6; CWL 4, 8.

[15] See the text cited at note 3 on page 20 above.

[16] *Development of Logic*, Oxford University Press, 1962, 96–100.

[17] Cf., for example, E. Mendelson, *Introduction to Mathematical Logic*; the axiom system for propositional calculus, p. 31, and first-order theories, p. 57.

[18] B. Lonergan, *op. cit.*, 4; CWL 4, 4.

[19] B. Lonergan, *Verbum: Word and Idea in Aquinas*, 55; CWL 2, 68. Cf. the index of this book under *syllogism, logic* and related topics.

[20] B. Lonergan, *Insight*, 280-1; CWL 3, 305–6.

[21] Cf. B. Lonergan, *Collection*, 5; CWL 4, 5–6.

[22] B. Lonergan, *Method in Theology*, London, 1972, 88, footnote 34; CWL 14, 85–85, footnote 55.

Chapter 9 ~ Aesthetico-Technic
Objectifications of Self-Assets

At the opposite extreme from mathematical expression stands the great phenomenon of artistic expression, the symbolization of vital and emotional experience for which verbal discourse is peculiarly unsuited. Epistemologically this sort of symbolic presentation has hardly been touched.[1]

In the last chapter, I dealt with symbolism in the context of a very specialized field within the intellectual pattern. We swing now to the other extreme to touch on certain aspects of symbolism in the context of total living. Just as in our discussion of logic in the previous chapter, so here in our discussion of living I do not aim at complete summary coverage: it is enough to try to orientate the reader to a proper approach to self-attentive methodology of this sphere, in particular the sphere of the arts. With that effort I associate the aim expressed somewhat as follows by Lonergan in a talk on art during a seminar on education:

> What I want to communicate in this talk on art is the notion that art is relevant to concrete living, that it is an exploration of the potentialities of concrete living, that it is extremely important in our age when philosophers for at least two centuries, through doctrines on economics, politics and education, have been trying to remake man and have done not a little to make human life unlivable.[2]

According to Stephen Ullman, emotive overtones in language are almost unavoidable except in treatises on logic and mathematics.[3] We move here then from the rare and exceptional sphere of the symbol as sign to the sphere where symbol is to be taken to mean affect-laden image.

The methodology of art within the works of Lonergan may be said to be largely a transformation of that of Susanne Langer.[4] That transformation can be missed in various ways which the attentive reader might possibly identify for himself immediately. In the first place, either one pursues this investigation through the well-defined scientific method of self-attention or one does not, and if one does not then one is liable to be tied to a refined description if not to a mere use of words. In the second place, the investigation and its conclusions must be consistently taken in the context of the realism of radical existentialism dealt with in the earlier chapters. The real is still, let me recall, what is to be reached by correct understanding. It is far from easy to pursue a discussion of art within that critical horizon. There is a constant gravitation toward taking the discussion to the obvious "realistic" level of the already-out-there-now. Thus I might write here, with Susanne Langer, of the piano as a living presence in room.5 I write, thus, meaning the real piano in the real room and its artistic import. But perhaps you find that spontaneously you think about the large brown object out there in the corner? You note that we are back at the problem of the Bridge of Asses of chapter five. There is an interesting relation between this Asses' Bridge and what Langer holds to be the Asses' Bridge of art theory. 6 The latter Asses' Bridge involved considering representation as nothing more than a device. Indeed, "The heavy leaning on the fruits of exact observation as symbols is merely one technique, one method of projecting the artists' inner world, among others."7 The reader should bring this problem back into the context of what was said toward the end of chapter five: the known elephant is not like the seen elephant! But the parallel is not quite as simple as that might suggest.

These are only hints, the primary purpose of which is to prevent you remaining within the grip of a naïve realism with regard to art and the discussion of art. Adequate understanding of art can be reached only within a larger methodological context than I have attempted to describe in this book, a context hinted at in the conclusion of these chapters and in the epilogue. Moreover, it involves serious engagement in some artistic modes. Nor, obviously, is such engagement enough. Even if we are not performers or writers, film and novel are modes of psychic liberation familiar to us all. But to specify with precision such familiar modes of being is quite another matter. Dancing may be a regular occurrence in your life, but a self-attentive appreciation of such an art form requires that performance be moved into the context of self-attentive methodology. Thus, "the almost universal confusion of self-expression with dance-expression, personal emotion with balletic emotion, is easy enough to understand if one considers the involved relations that dance really has to feeling and its bodily symptoms."8 "To keep virtual elements and actual materials separate is not easy for anyone without philosophical training. ... It takes precision of thought not to confuse an imagined feeling, or a precisely conceived emotion that is formulated in a perceptible symbol, with a feeling or emotion actually experienced in response to real events. Indeed, the very notion of feelings and emotions not really felt, but only imagined, is strange to most people."9

With this quotation I have rather abruptly plunged the reader into a complex theory of art. Still, the plunge can be wholesome, bringing you perhaps to a particular realization of what we talked about in general in chapter one, a realization of the need for, a refined type of reflection on all the patterns of experience of contemporary society if man is to get to grips with his own renewal. One might consider present orientation in dance forms in this light, recalling that "the dance often reaches the zenith of its development in the primitive stage of a culture when other arts are just dawning on its ethnic horizon,"[10] also considering the secularization of the dance,[11] its particular mode as virtual gesture of power, its relation to the problem mentioned by Lonergan of liberation of consciousness within the contemporary scene.

Let us return now from these hints and wider considerations to bring you to some notion of the underlying view of art. Need I recall here the story of the physicist and the lady?

I can state briefly then that art involves the objectification of a purely experiential pattern. Here let us tease out slowly what is meant by that. First of all, we will slip over the word "pattern," assuming that you are familiar with it in its normal usage. The pattern in question here is experiential, auditory, visual, motor, etc. It is purely experiential, of the seen as seen, etc. One can best indeed understand "purely" as qualifying the complex expression "experiential pattern." There is involved, then, both an exclusion and an inclusion. There is involved an exclusion of alien patterns and influences that instrumentalize experience. Such alien patterns and influences can be practical, scientific, philosophic, or motivational. Most evident is the practical influence: then, for example, seeing red is instrumental to putting on the brake, hearing a bell may be instrumental to downing tools. Less evident is the motivational: one can go to an art exhibition and look long merely because it is the thing to do.

But the inclusion is the positive and important element here. The inclusion connotes that the seen is seen and the heard is heard with all its associations, spontaneously. One may note that this does not exclude a didactic component, but that component must have the quality of spontaneity, it must not be an imposed alien pattern. Again, the inclusion goes deeper. There is on the level of the psyche an orientation which, as it were, resonates with the orientation of man's intelligence that is expressed in questions, in wonder. With that orientation is associated feelings of fascination.[12] "Purely experiential pattern" connotes a liberation of that orientation, a relief and an openness, an expansion along the lines of its own proper rhythm. I recall here Charles Morgan's description of the function of dramatic art, extending its application to other forms of art:

> Dramatic art has a double function—first still the preoccupied mind, to empty it of triviality, to make it receptive and meditative: then to impregnate it. Illusion is the impregnating power. It is that spiritual force in dramatic art which impregnates the silence of the spectator, enabling him to perceive or imagine.[13]

There is a lifting of the person out of the ready-made world, a translation from the pressures of home and office, economics and politics, from the time of daily doing to the time of music, from the print and prose of news and science to language no longer instrument of literal meaning but pool of psychic possibilities. It is a withdrawal from practicality to an exploration of the possibilities of living in a richer world. Debussy put the point well when he remarked, writing to Stravinsky, "For me it is a special satisfaction to tell you how much you have enlarged the boundaries of the permissible in the empire of sound."[14] One might say that just as the mathematician explores possibilities relevant to science, so the artist explores the potentialities of total human living. All living involves artistry, is dramatic, but art focuses in its objectification of purely experiential patterns a possibility of fuller living, more integral meaning. Depending on the state of a culture, that objectification can be expressive of a rich common meaning and a common aspiration, or on the other hand, it can include elements of "shock," artistic isolation,[15] entombment in museums, liturgy without light or life.

I have said that art involves the objectification of a purely experiential pattern, but as yet I have not discussed objectification. In her later work Langer has a long discussion of the projection of feeling in art,[16] and I make no attempt to reproduce that treatment or its larger and essential context. But let me give some indications.

So far we have been dealing in a general way rather with what is projected and also received according to the responsiveness of the public.[17] It is within the context of this prior discussion that one might treat of the identity of known and knower, of seen and seer, etc. One talks of a work of art as being dynamic, alive, but it is you, the perceiver, the listener, that is alive and coming to life. But there is the transition from identity to expression involved in objectification which in many ways parallels the objectification which occurs on the level of intellect. Here I will emphasize, in the manner which should prove helpful, one parallel, by relating the treatment here of objectification to what was said in the preceding chapter about symbolic technique involving a certain objectification of mind. Before touching on that parallel I must recall what was already mentioned in our earlier quotations concerning the dance, that the expression in art is not spontaneous self-expression, it is "emotion recollected in tranquility." There is involved a detachment of the artist from himself, the introduction of what might be called psychic distance. The objectification involves, too, a mediation of total mind, an appreciation of significance, an idealization of the purely experiential pattern. There is an unfolding, a revealing, of import, detached from the accidentals of concrete experience. But the detachment from accidentals is not an abstraction yielding formulation: The pattern cannot be conceptualized.

Now it is of great interest to note here that much of this has been said perhaps better and at greater length elsewhere. But saying and meaning are different things. What I mean, for example, by asserting the impossibility, of conceptualization involves a context of self-attentive methodology. The meaning of conceptualization involves the meaning of intelligible emanations, of understanding and its expression, a meaning reached only insofar as one scientifically attends in one's own performance to the processes of insight and formulation and the transition from one to the other.

We may turn now to the question of a partial parallel between the last chapter and this by considering the following quotation:

> In actual felt activity the form is elusive, for it collapses into a condensed and foreshortened memory almost as fast as the experience passes; to hold and contemplate it requires an image which can be held for contemplation, But there is no simple image of our inner dynamism as there is of visually perceived forms and colours and sound patterns. A symbol capable of articulating the forms of feelings is, therefore, necessarily presented in some sort of projection as an extraorganic structure that conveys the movement of emotive and perceptive processes. Such a projection is a work of art. It presents the semblance of feeling so directly to logical intuition that we seem to perceive feeling itself in the work; but of course the work does not contain feeling, any more than a proposition about the mortality of Socrates contains a philosopher.[18]

A preliminary remark recalls the warning earlier in this chapter about naïve realism. Langer points out at one stage that "'space-tension' is an attribute belonging only to virtual space, where *esse est percipi*."[19] This statement might usefully be considered here and also linked with the earlier remarks about the identity of known and knower, and objectification. The virtual space, the space of the picture, is not more out-there than real space is. In paradoxical and question-raising fashion I might add, of course, that it is, in a certain sense, more out-there: I leave the reader to sort that out. Again, whether one is reading sentences in a book of science or in a book of poetry, there is to be distinguished the print as seen and the real print. The real print is not *like* the seen print: the real print, as in the case of anything real, is to be known through correct understanding. Not that correctly understanding the nature of real print is the scientific reader's aim is to understand what is meant, what is written about. The reader of the written work of art, however, is not operating in that intellectual pattern. He or she is orientated toward that total response that I have been describing. Because of this the print and the sound are not just media for the understanding of something, as they are for the scientific reader. They are responded to in ways I have been trying to indicate in this chapter.

At all events it is insofar as you think within the context of the realism of radical existentialism that you will grasp correctly what is going on, what is meant in particular by the concluding sentence of the lengthy quotation above from Susanne Langer. And in that context, you must stay if the parallel I make between symbolic logic and the art-logic is not to be misunderstood or understood mythically. Like symbolic logic, the art-work is a "moving object" for the human subject, but in a different pattern, a total pattern. Again, just as symbolic logic has developed in complexity and technique, embodying in apt symbolism the strategies of contemporary implication, etc., so art and artistry develop in complexity and technique, embodying in apt "extraorganic structures" the artistic import. But in contrast with symbolic logic, that "extraorganic structure" is not merely an objectification of mind, but an objectification of man and his human possibilities. I leave the reader to exploit the parallels thus briefly indicated, to push them as far as they will go, to pick out their inadequacies. You could for a start return to the quotation from Langer which I have given and read it in reference to the previous chapter, replacing the word "feeling" in it by the word "thought."

Furthermore, the parallels indicated are not restricted to symbolic logic. Besides the apt symbolism there is the computer, besides logical systems there is technology. Moreover, the wider objectification of mind connoted here involves not merely logic but science, not merely science but philosophy and theology, not merely philosophy and theology as conventionally conceived but philosophy and theology in their anthropological turn, in their scientific cultivation of self-assets. And while man has indeed his Inner Mansions in those assets, still he and his loved ones must live in some resonance with their surrounds, with a national and global credit or debt in the objectification of the wealth of man. I have not enlarged here on axial objectifications but perhaps at least the reader begins to see the link-up between science, technology and art, and the influence for better or worse of a philosophy or a theology on science, technology and art. If a man is a machine, then all that is required is a greater machine in which he may fit as a cog. If man is conceived to any extent as a machine, there will be an ever-present tendency to fit him in as a cog. But man is not a machine. To treat here of the hierarchy of integrated aggregates and the unified levels of orientations that is man would be impossible. But common sense and art cling to what theory seeks to grasp: man does not take kindly to being, considered a machine. Furthermore, not only is human intelligence and will radically beyond the mechanical, man's entire conscious life reflects the radicality to challenge any form of biochemical, neural or cultural determinism. There is an axial demand for liberation not only on the level of mind but on the level, too, of feeling. But more of this in the epilogue.

I have touched here on the clash between psychic orientation and wrong explanation. But neither is correct explanation, even human living: "Explanation does not give a man a home."[20] There is needed not merely fire and shelter but a home and a hearth, not merely food for the mind and organs but for the psyche. Such are the needs of living, and their neglect within a culture can be mirrored in a failure within education for living.

> Artistic training is, therefore, the education of feeling, as our usual schooling in factual subjects, and logical skill such as mathematical "figuring" or simple argumentation (principles are hardly even explained), is the education of thought. Few people realize that the real education of emotion is not the "conditioning" effected by social approval and disapproval, but the tacit, personal, illuminating contact with symbols of feeling. Art education, therefore, is neglected, left to chance, or regarded as a cultural veneer.[21]

But besides the education of the child there is the education and continued orientation of the adult, the education of a people. That education requires the orientation and reach of artistry, and it has as many modes as the modes of artistry. We might survey briefly some of these modes, treated at length by Susanne Langer, especially in *Feeling and Form*.

There is the painting, which draws man out of the weary space of common life into a virtual space, a space which is not real, which is not measured by the steps of the fly walking on the canvas. There is music, song, and poetry, which open man to his history and his potentialities, which reveal to him through layers of resonances the meaning of his life, his people. There is the lyric, expressive of the individual subject, and the drama, expressive of the destiny of the group. One can think here not only of the more remote and refined symphony or opera, but of the ballad, the wartime songs, the immediately popular songs. It is in such regions that one may find the soul of a people, their common meaning. In this context one might consider, for example, daily and weekly papers and magazines with their offer of minimal meaning.

Then there is sculpture in general, which "effects the objectification of self and environment for the sense of sight."[22] There is the statue and there is architecture, and these are related to each other as the lyric and the drama. While the statue is a visual presentation of the space that feels which is man, architecture is expressive of the orientation of a people. "The primary illusion of plastic art, *virtual space*, appears in architecture as *envisagement of an ethnic domain*."[23] The reader should consider in this light, and in the context of radical realism for which the real is not just the seen, the objectification of human meaning which is the city. It is the product of meaning and meaninglessness, with street names and structures echoing the existential memory and orientation of the people. That dialectic of meaning and meaninglessness may have left the city soulless, its heart the haunt of admen, pulsing with hazy movement, encompassed by beige suburban dullness.

But the dialectic continues and to that dialectic the present chapter is a contribution. I have been content here to emphasize the importance of art and to indicate the way in which it might be reflected upon in self-attentive manner. Nonetheless, with the innovation of longer cycle, which this book is about, comes the probability of a deeper transformation of art. Just as electronics enlarge the possibilities of sound, and optics give rise to a widening field of op-art, so the self-digestion of self-assets that will slowly emerge from serious self-attention can give rise to an epochal novelty of art, a new dimension in the daily drama of survival.

But is there not a touch of unreality about all this cultivation of interiority and aesthetic in the face of what are evident needs of the Great Ascent? There is a Malthusian shadow over the crops of 1973.

Heilbroner in *The Great Ascent* dispatches with simple views of development and provision.[24] In this present book I seek to help the reader dispatch with simple views of what it is to have a view. Certainly there is a need for bread. But that need can be met only through the mediation of mind in a range of sciences and techniques. And my thesis is that this mediation of mind itself needs minding, if we are to survive genuinely and not just with an abundance of bread.

Notes

[1] Susanne Langer, *Mind: An Essay on Human Feeling*, I, Baltimore, Johns Hopkins University Press, 1967, 80. This book is henceforth referred to as Langer, 1967.

[2] *Topics in Education*, Collected Works of Bernard Lonergan, vol. 10, Robert Doran and Frederick Crowe (eds.), University of Toronto Press, 1993, p. 232.

[3] *The Principles of Semantics*, Oxford, Blackwell, 1963, 13.

[4] Especially contained in *Feeling and Form*, London, Routledge, 1953, to be referred to below as Langer, 1953.

[5] Langer, 1953, 100, footnote.

[6] Langer, 1967, 97, footnote.

[7] L. Lewisohn, *The Permanent Horizon: A New Search for Old Truths*, New York, Harper, 1934, 134.

[8] Langer, 1953, 183.

[9] Ibid., 181.

[10] Ibid., ix.

[11] Ibid., 187, 492 ff.

[12] One might draw here on Rudolph Otto's little book *The Idea of the Holy* but not, of course, on his deficient realism.

[13] See "The Nature of Dramatic Illusion," in *Essays by Divers Hands: Transactions of the Royal Society of Literature*, edited by R. W. Macan, Oxford University Press, 1933, 70.

[14] Quoted in Donald Mitchell's *The Language of Modern Music*, London, Faber, 1966, 22.

[15] The little work by Donald Mitchell just cited illustrates this element of shock and isolation well, for example, in the case of Schoenberg.

[16] Langer, 1967, 4.

[17] Langer, 1953, 396 ff.

[18] Langer, 1967, 67.

[19] Langer, 1953, 371.

[20] Lonergan, *Insight*, 547; CWL 3, 570.

[21] Langer, 1953, 401.

[22] Langer, 1953, 91.

[23] Langer, 1953, 100; italics in text.

[24] He does so more vigorously in *The Human Prospect*. But may I recall here my comments in chapter 1 regarding the longer cycle and axial innovation? Human inventiveness is both unimaginable and unpredictable. I do not share his gloom.

Chapter 10 ~ The Notion of Survival

It must be clear that the first essential is not a change in policy so much as a change in point of view. We must lift ourselves out of our accustomed American frame of reference and catapult ourselves across a distance wider than the oceans that separate us from the continents in which the struggle for development is taking place. To repeat a phrase we have used more than once, we must learn to see the Great Ascent as it is, and not as we would like it to be.[1]

But is it clear that a change in point of view is essential? To me it is more than sufficiently clear: Is it to you? I would like, then, my reader to sit back and entertain the question with me from various aspects. There is a paradox here, relating to the reliability of my guidelines, which I will deal with briefly in concluding this chapter: the need for change in point of view is thoroughly clear only from a changed point of view. My introductory book is an effort to give guidelines to that change in point of view. And my problem, as I move to conclusion, is to preserve the introductory perspective while yet giving intimations of the promised view. The intimations I leave to the epilogue: let me here round off the introduction with some further pointers.

The invitation has been to lift oneself out of one's accustomed frame of reference through self-attention. Our concern has been not directly the Great Ascent as Heilbroner conceives it but the axis of the Great Ascent. In more technical terms our concern has been precisely foundational, where Heilbroner's concern is more related to policy, planning, and execution.

> Corresponding to doctrines, systematics and communications in theological method, integrated studies would distinguish policy making, planning, and the execution of the plans. Policy is concerned with attitudes and ends. Planning works out the optimal use of existing resources for attaining the ends under given conditions. Execution generates feedback. This supplies scholars and scientists with the data for studies on the wisdom of policies and the efficacy of the planning. The result of such attention to feedback will be that policy making and planning become ongoing processes that are continuously revised in the light of their consequences.[2]

This is not to say that Heilbroner's interests are not also foundational—I have already noted his comment on the absence of methodological concern[3]—but his interest does not blossom into the identification of a well-defined science of the self. And "to see The Great Ascent as it is," one must raise the question, "Who am I, Who are we that ascend?" and one must reach some axial answers. Furthermore, though there is at present a growing literature[4] on the topic of *Future Shock*,[5] the horizons of discussion are regularly only those of common sense and science.

Still, perhaps, that interest, that literature, and that discussion could ground some agreement with the economist Kenneth Boulding's remark, "The fact of the great transition is not in dispute."[6] What will be in dispute is the specification I have given the transition. So, before concluding with summary indication of the total dimensions of that transition let me add persuasive witness to the economic aspect of it by a brief consideration of the work of Adolph Lowe *On Economic Knowledge*.[7] It is the fruit of forty years of inquiry into the matter and method of economics which I take here as a pre-axial replacement in the twentieth century of Smith's *The Wealth of Nations*. Let me indicate immediately what I mean.

Every academic, as every man, has a history. In the introduction I made an attempt to indicate that briefly for some of those who were thinking and writing in 1773. But obviously the indication would need to be enlarged on: the student days at Edinburgh of David Hume; Glasgow University some fifteen years later (1737–40) where Smith studied under Francis Hutcheson; the Konigsberg of Kant's initiation into Wolff and Newton by Martin Knutzen in 1740, the year Smith moved to Balliol in Oxford, where things had reached such a philosophic pass that Smith was nearly sent down because a copy of David Hume's *A Treatise of Human Nature* was found in his rooms. And so on: but most of all, one would need to get to grips with what I would call the Newtonian Mood of the times.[8]

Now the Newtonian Mood is still with us. By this I do not mean that Newtonian theory is still with us: in fact it is, for it is a highly successful approximative theory. Nor do I mean that the Newtonian approach is still relevant: it is, where by the Newtonian approach I mean the performance of Newton, as also the performances of Brahe and Kepler. But what I mean by Newtonian mood is much more related to speech about the performances, where the speech tends to be more about Newton's performance than Kepler's, more about Newton's deductions than of his discoveries.

Nor did Adolph Lowe escape the Newtonian mood of the universities of Munich, Berlin, and Tübingen during his studies in law, economics, and philosophy in the beginning of this century.[9] Forty years of reflection within this mood as crystallized in twentieth-century methodology of science have led him from the question, "How is a theory of the business cycle possible?"[10] to a more fundamental questioning of the possibility of economic theory. But what is really in question is the Newtonian mood, what is really emerging is an axial interest.

Summary is normally illusory, but some hints may help.

Lowe begins his discussion by noting that "there is far-reaching agreement among philosophers and methodologists as to what constitutes a fully developed 'science,'[11] and he draws on Ernest Nagel, *The Structure of Science*,[12] for definition. The agreed constitution is fundamentally that of the hypothetico-deductive method, and for the remainder of the book Lowe struggles to enlarge its meaning sufficiently to allow political economy the name of science. He argues excellently toward his view of instrumental inference[13] but on the way the axial question is raised: The principles and pattern of his approach are "the result of an inference. How is this type of inference to be defined?"[14] We are back at the basic issue of the present book: inferences and insights are events; they can be named initially much as we name plants at the beginning of botany; they can be investigated through generalized empirical method;[15] they can be defined "not without labor"[16] in a manner which meets the epistemological and methodological issues of our time.

There follows in Lowe, in part three, a discussion of the historical trend of economic science during the 200 years on which my introduction focused, which helps to concretize for the beginner the project of metaphysics. Not only does metaphysics include heuristically economics and history, but also the history of economic science.

Of the many worthwhile points in Lowe's final exposition of his view in part four, I will note only three which are suggestive both for specialist and non-specialist. First of all, there is the clear parallel between Lowe's three steps relating to Controlled Economic systems and the distinctions noted above.[17]

> The first is *political:* postulation of a macro-goal and of the qualifying criteria to define the over-all purpose of economic activity. The second is *scientific:* instrumental elaboration of the system's path, of the behavioral and motivational patterns, and of specific measures of Control, all of which are to be suitable to transform the initial state into a terminal state of goal-adequacy. The third step is *administrative:* application of the measures of Control as derived by instrumental

analysis to the actual regulation of the structure and, above all, of the dynamic forces of the system.[18]

But note immediately the difference, a difference perhaps difficult to accept: we are back at the issue of horizons. The meaning of Lonergan's last three functional specialties is reached after prolonged self-attentive inquiry into insight; what Lowe means by his three steps is limited by what he means by inference.

My second point carries this difference to the broader issue of control.

> Stated in the simplest terms the issue is now one of finding a substitute for the impersonal factors of the environment—pressures and resource mobility—a substitute capable of inducing motivational and behavioral patterns which assure good working order under the changed conditions. Such a substitute can only be a personified force, henceforth denoted as *Control.*[19]

Lowe immediately relates Control to public policy, but his developed view requires "the formation of enlightened public opinion capable of understanding the primary Control."[20] Now, in discussing horizons I indicated the axial transition, as the concrete possibility of a shift from spontaneous use of intelligence to guided use.[21] While I have not dealt in this short book with the complex topic of meaning, I wish now to add that what is involved is a radical change in the control of meaning, and "if social and cultural changes are, at root, changes in meanings that are grasped and accepted, changes in the control of meaning mark off the great epochs in human history."[22]

Perhaps at this stage what is meant by specifying Lowe's book as a pre-axial replacement of *The Wealth of Nations* begins to emerge? Nor is this a belittling of Lowe's work, which focuses so clearly on present needs. Indeed, his closing perspective meshes with the present concern, when he takes as yardstick "the elevation of microautonomy itself to the rank of a genuine goal."[23] What lifts the yardstick to axiality is the conception, affirmation, and implementation of microautonomy within metaphysics.

At this stage in my concluding chapter there is the impossibility of broadening out into a *Concluding Unscientific Postscript to the Philosophical Fragments* [24] I have so far presented. With Kenneth Boulding I might assert that "this happens to be my planet and I am very much attached to it, and I am desperately anxious that this particular experiment should be a success."[25] In that same context Boulding speaks of an "invisible college" which might share his view.

Frankly I place more hope in Galbraith's Academic Estate[26] and within that Estate in those beyond their teens still with a creative suspicion of contemporary ills and possibilities and a spark of authentic radical revolution. In an earlier work I wrote, "One must think concretely here of the botanist on the campus with commitments to professional reading, publication, teaching, socializing, and, underpinning all these, not the notion of being but the notion of surviving."[27] But here I am concerned with the notion of survival not in that popular sense but in the strict sense that identifies it with the notion of being, and in the less strict sense that identifies it with the incarnate you in your possibilities of *super-vivere*, peak-living.[28]

In the strict sense the notion of survival is that core of you that I have invited you to question in the early chapters.

The invitation spread more to the looser sense when we turned to the technico-aesthetic you. But our honest question now must be, "Did you read me, loud and clear?" We are back with the problem of the preface, the problem of reading without "minding."[29] We are back at the introduction with Kant's request to "make many careful observations."

Is it one thing to read, "Make many careful observations" and still another to undertake the observations? That depends on the reader. If one is seriously searching for the mountaintop, the sight of the signpost is the beginning of the climb. I have been signposting you into what may seem a mist for over a hundred pages. "Our partly socialized capitalism is an unstable mixture of conflicting principles, a halfway house from which we must go forward in one direction or the other."[30] But here my manifesto has been neither capitalist nor communist: It has been concerned with the deeper issue of another halfway house,[31] a left-wing realism, a radical existentialism, a metaprinciple to guide that going forward. Our twentieth-century political structures have emerged in these last centuries from a geography and history of spontaneous insights. To speak of some overarching Hegelian dialectic—leftwing or not—is just silly. Nor is there anything inevitable in the manner in which black, brown, and yellow peoples may contribute to give our globe a gayer color in these next few centuries. My manifesto is for some few to go to the root of spontaneous intelligence to bring forth in patience a deeper measure of control.

But perhaps I am deluded in my suggestion of an innovation of longer cycle? Perhaps there is too much risk and mist, not to speak of error, in my particular signposting? And are there not other views with more to offer? The question is yours and, as I have noted elsewhere, the answer lies in the anthropological turn. Process theology provides an insightful world-view—but if it includes the subject, does it include the subject that I am, that I might be? Analytic philosophy exercises my intelligence and judgment—but can it coherently clarify the exclusion of my curiosity regarding that exercise? And so on, in a dialectic of performance and consent.[32]

To elaborate on that intimate dialectic of the human subject and its refinement through novel aesthetico-technic feedback would call for a further and axial work. However, for the beginner who is with me so far it is evident, even descriptively, that there is something odd, say, in the performance of a reviewer of the present book who would claim that my understanding of human knowing is incorrect. For is not his claim a knowing? Is it not perhaps even a claim to a correct understanding?

This basic thesis then is not descriptively elusive. More elusive is the total import of the axial claim. That axial claim centers attention on the mind of man, intentional existence.[33] Through a million years of feeling, understanding, commitment, and education there is given on the globe a rich deposit in the minds of modern men: the deposit of their understanding. That understanding is of sticks and stones, fossils and flowers, moon rockets and merchandise. But it is a deposit that is data: For that range of specimens of understanding coterminous with the scientific and the commonsense insights of the present human group have still to be named, classified, attended to, understood, heuristically conceived. It is that beginning of an understanding of understanding that can put the globe on a new axis.

And now I hope I have succeeded in indicating just how definitely we are at a beginning and only at a beginning. The possibility of intentional existence—Aquinas's *potens omnia fieri*[34]—is the subject's possibility to be focal-fashion all that he or she is not. Not to in some way attend to that possibility is opting for what Heidegger calls a forgetfulness of being. To attend seriously to that realm, that notion of survival which is you at core but also you in kilos, is to open yourself to a new vision of the globe with its natural rhythms overlaced and orbited by man-made assets. A final paragraph in an introductory book is no place to treat of the contrast between *ens extensum* and *intentio entis*.[35] Popularly put, you are larger than the Red Square, taller than Manhattan, deeper than galactic space. Not to contemplate that aspirative universe within is much more than a sorry personal loss.

Notes

¹ Robert L. Heilbroner, *The Great Ascent*, 148.

² B. Lonergan, *Method in Theology*, 365–66; CWL 14, 337.

³ See chapter five, conclusion. The quotation is from an essay on Adolph Lowe's *On Economic Knowledge. Towards a Science of Political Economics*, New York, Harper and Row, 1965, a book we will consider presently. Heilbroner, in the same volume, considers various other views on economic science. Again, Heilbroner's *The Limits of American Capitalism*, New York, Harper and Row, 1967, brings out the need for Foundations in Lonergan's sense.

⁴ For a bibliography see V. C. Fergiss, *Technological Man: The Myth and the Reality*, New York, Braziller, 1969.

⁵ The title of the best seller by Alvin Toler. My Bantam edition, 1972, is a nineteenth printing, an indication of contemporary need.

⁶ Kenneth E. Boulding, *The Meaning of the Twentieth Century: The Great Transition*, New York, Harper and Row, 1965, 180.

⁷ See endnote 3 above.

⁸ I recall here "the menace of experiential conjugation" in philosophy (see *Plants and Pianos*, 16 ff.). A general comment may help beginners locate themselves. One may easily use the phrase "Newtonian mood" but to enter serious meta-discussion of the topic requires as a minimum some familiarity, e.g., with the integration of the Newtonian equations of motion. Recall my earlier comment on apology in philosophy (see p. 2) and on the problem of the heuristic definition of development, be the development botanical, economic, or doctrinal (see p. 59). The paradigm case for "the menace of experiential conjugation" might well be taken to be the possibility of methodological talk about space-time in the absence of knowledge of both physics and interiority.

⁹ Lowe's indications of indebtedness in the preface and in footnotes, in fact, raises the wider question of the dialectic of the Newtonian mood and the *Geisteswissenschaften*, a non-introductory question involving a discussion of meaning which I have avoided here.

¹⁰ "*Wie ist Konjunkturtheorie überhaupt maglich?*" *Weltwirtschaftliches Archiv*, 24, (1926).

¹¹ *On Economic Knowledge*, 4, footnote 1.

¹² New York, Harcourt, 1961.

¹³ *Op. cit.*, 128–61.

¹⁴ Ibid., 140.

¹⁵ B. Lonergan, *Insight*, 72, section 1.1; CWL 3, 95–6. The phenomenological movement has succeeded in revealing some of the complex riches of this area but

its essential lack is a precise exploration and exploitation of the phenomenon of inner is-saying.

[16] B. Lonergan, *Verbum: Word and Idea in Aquinas*, Notre Dame, 1967, 25; CWL 2, 38.

[17] See endnote 2 above. There is a further parallel which is worth pointing out even though it is too complex to elaborate on here and besides one term of the comparison, B. Lonergan's *Circulation Analysis*, a 130-page typescript produced in the early forties, is unpublished. [It is now published as "Part Three: Circulation Analysis" in *For a New Political Economy*, vol. 21, Collected Works of Bernard Lonergan, ed. Philip McShane, Toronto, University of Toronto Press, 1998, pp. 231–318.] The other term of comparison is Lowe's work on the interrelated circulations of levels of production (*On Economic Knowledge*, 268 ff.; "A Structural Model of Production," *Social Research*, 1952, 135-76). There are parallels between their divisions of sectors and their analyses of cross-over requirements, but Lonergan's discussion would seem to have "more bones"—to recall endnote 7 of chapter 3 above—and its placing of Control is significantly different, a difference relating to our topic of axiality.

[18] *Op. cit.*, 156–57.

[19] Ibid., 130.

[20] Ibid., 283.

[21] See endnote 15 on page 7 above.

[22] B. Lonergan, "Dimensions of Meaning," *Collection*, Herder and Herder, New York, 1967, 255–56; CWL 4, 235.

[23] Lowe, *op. cit.*, 318.

[24] The title is Kierkegaard's. I may remark here that while radical existentialism may owe more than its name to the tradition associated with Kierkegaard, it belongs to a longer and more significant tradition. Undoubtedly Kierkegaard can discuss topics like despair with more psychic vigor than is evident in the questions on it in Aquinas's *Summa*, but I incline to rank Aquinas's achievements and suggestiveness higher. The modern Thomist, however, imitates the master better if topics such as dread, satire, despair, are moved into the complex interiority context indicated in the epilogue. Dread has its electrochemical aspects.

[25] *The Meaning of the Twentieth Century*, 192.

[26] *The New Industrial State*, chapter XXV ff. The longer cycle of our suggested innovation requires of course a root questioning of the structures and institutions of education from pre-kindergarten to post-research, but the present schemes of recurrence seem most open to fruitful change at the level indicated.

[27] *Plants and Pianos*, 50. Relevant here is A. Maslow, *The Psychology of Science*, Chicago, Gateway, 1969, chapter 3, where he discusses "The Cognitive Needs Under Conditions of Fear and of Courage."

[28] I would recall here Maslow's two books, *Toward a Psychology of Being*, Princeton, NJ, Van Nostrand, 1962, and *Religions, Values, and Peak Experiences*, New York, Viking Press, 1970.

[29] I recall here Gaston Bachelard's remark, "Every book should be re-read as soon as it is finished. After the sketchiness of the first reading comes the creative work of reading. We must then know the *problem* that confronted the author. The second, then the third reading . . . give us, little by little, the solution of this problem" (*The Poetics of Space*, Boston, Beacon Press, 1970, 21). Relevant also are his comments on "reading" a house, a box, a nest (*ibid.*, 14, 39, 47, 83).

[30] Louis Kelso and Mortimer Adler, *The Capitalist Manifesto*, New York, Random House, 1958, in the preface by Mortimer Adler, xvi.

[31] B. Lonergan, *Insight*, xxviii; CWL 3, 22.

[32] B. Lonergan, *Introducing the Thought of Bernard Lonergan*, Darton, Longman and Todd, London, 1973, in the introduction by P. McShane, 12. I take advantage of the reference to note an error on the same page: Lonergan's stay at Harvard was from 1971 to 1972.

[33] B. Lonergan, *Verbum*, 151; CWL 2, 162.

[34] *Ibid.*, 85 ff.; CWL 2, 96–7.

[35] Extended being and the notion of being. Prime matter and prime mind are both possibilities of multibeing: but what radically different possibilities, what radically different evaluations of Gross National Product they ground!

Epilogue: Being and Loneliness[1]

> . . . each member, each group, indeed our whole host and its great pilgrimage, was only a wave in the eternal stream of human beings, of the eternal strivings of the human spirit towards the East, towards Home. . . .[2]

The topic I have taken here is one I understand only in heuristic obscurity: What I say is mainly a searching, a looking forward. The dimensions of that looking forward may gradually peep out as outrageously beyond our timely conception, But for the moment let us turn to some questions of context.

I will touch on five contexts: a philosophic context, the personal context, an aesthetic context, the methodological context and, finally a religious context. It is only in the religious context that the question raised by the topic "Being and Loneliness" locates itself precisely in a beatific quest,[3] but as we move through contexts I will touch on various contemporary expressions of that quest, and the possible methodological reorientation of such expressed quests. My reflections in fact are more methodological than theological, and therefore have more than theistic appeal. The main focus of attention may, indeed, be considered to be the task of cultivating an authentic humanism in a world in which, to recall remarks of Lonergan quoted earlier, [4] for centuries philosophers, economists, and politicians have made human life barely livable.

But that problem of dehumanization has not escaped serious thinkers. It did not escape Harnack when he noted that men have been trapped in work clothes for centuries. It did not escape Rilke when he sought a recollection from technicity of man, as open, through poetry. It did not escape Husserl when he criticized emergent patterns of modern sciences. It did not escape Maslow when he pointed out how few adults reach maturity. It did not escape Aresteh when he sought for a normative theory of genuine adult growth.

Yet, while such men help to specify a context, the philosophic context for my consideration of "Being and Loneliness" is reached by its titular relationship with four efforts of the present century to grapple with the problem, the efforts namely of Marcel, de Finance, Heidegger and Sartre under the respective titles *Being and Having, Being and Doing, Being and Time, Being and Nothingness.* Clearly, the task of interpreting these men, systematically expressing the root of their problematic, and indicating a growth pattern from the root which would be, not dark, but lightsome—with a light not just eternal but radically and immediately human[5]—that task is not for a day but a decade. So, in this epilogue one can expect only tidbits of the task to emerge. Here, however, I would like to note an obvious and essential point: that these thinkers are authentically unusual. I recall Jung's remark that the truly contemporary man is alone—and the aloneness here is an aloneness of meaning. I recall Friedrich Schlegel's view: "A classic is a writing that is never fully understood. But those that are educated and educate themselves must always want to learn more from it."[6] More artistically, Antoine de Saint-Exupery remarks: "No single event can awake within us a stranger totally unknown to us. To live is to be slowly born. It would be a bit too easy if we could go about borrowing ready-made souls."[7] I recall, too, the shrewd saying of Lao Tzu:

> Not to value the teacher,
> Nor to love the material,
> Though it seems clever, betrays great bewilderment.
> This is called the essential and the secret.[8]

Finally, there is the more elaborate comment of Bernard Lonergan on the same topic:

> The major texts, in classics, in religion, letters, philosophy, theology, not only are beyond the initial horizon of their interpreters but also may demand an intellectual, moral, religious conversion of the interpreter over and above the broadening of his horizon.
>
> In this case the interpreter's initial knowledge of the object is just inadequate. He will come to know it only in so far as he pushes the self-correcting process of learning to a revolution in his own outlook. He can succeed in acquiring that habitual understanding of an author that spontaneously finds his wave-length and locks on it, only after he has effected a radical change in himself.
>
> This is the existential dimension of the problem of hermeneutics.[9]

To emphasize this existential dimension, we may move immediately to the personal context, the context of you and I raising questions about ourselves and our concerns.

How many of us, then, have felt profoundly—and I use the word "felt" deliberately—the problem that Heidegger raises at the beginning of *Being and Time*, the problem of the "forgetfulness of Being"? How many of us, with Sartre, have been pierced with the "nothingness lying coiled in the heart of being—like a worm"?[10] or being hounded by the reality of ourselves, each for-itself, as "an always future hollow"?[11] Which of us can stand authentically with

Camus and claim that "it takes ten years to get an idea"? Not many of us can take as our own Marcel's words, ". . . the thinker on the other hand is continually on guard against the alienation (through inertia), the fossilization of his thought. He lives in a continual state of creativity and the whole of his thought is always called in question from one minute to the next."[12] How few of us, perhaps, will walk with Husserl in middle age with the longing he expressed to Brentano: "How I would like to live on the heights. For this is all my thinking craves for. But shall I ever work my way upwards, if only for a little, so that I can gain something of a free distant view? I am now forty-five years old and am still a miserable beginner."[13] And none of us could dare hope to slump into silence with Aquinas near the end with the deeply authentic comment on a life of growing understanding, "It is all straw."

But let me move back from commenting on an intellectual giant to a more comforting comment regarding aesthetic context.

Intellectual genius is rare, as is aesthetic genius. But to aesthetic genius there is a wider possibility of human response. The understanding of that possibility lies in an adequate theory of the embodiment of the infinite hollowness or project which is *Dasein*, but the feeling for it is as evident as the gap between sensed sunshine and a theory of heat.[14] So, the recitation of a theology of the incarnation (even if heard understandingly, not merely nominalistically) may leave us cold, while a choirful of O'Riada's "Ag Críost an Síol" may touch us to the core. Again, the classroom question, "Who am I?" may be merely something to be noted down, remembered, while the same question as posed in such simple aesthetic form as Neil Diamond's song "Holly Holy" in which occurs the phrase, "where I am, what I am, what I believe in" can call forth resonances ranging from phosphate variations in calf muscle to the loneliness and love of intertwining persons, and even beyond, to piety suspecting a call to holiness.

Nor, obviously, do I select the question, "Who am I?" at random. For if it is pursued authentically in the coolness of intelligence[15] it moves one to a core heuristic answer to the question "What is Being?" But we speak now not of an intellectual pursuit but of an incarnate resonance. And that incarnate response comes forth from the incarnate hollow at the call of meaning. It comes forth, as Sartre would say, from human reality as "a lack . . . haunted in its inmost being by the being of what it desires."[16] There would be no response if there were no desire, no questing. But is the desire, the lack, fulfilled by this response? Are we satiated by the duration of a song? We would not want, except in poetry,

> . . . over and over,
> To listen to the song for ever in blessed pain,
> To the song that could make me happy, tangled in
> your delicate hands.[17]

Are we not rather, in Sartre's words, "an always future hollow"? The quest, "Who am I?" that man embodies (within the core quest of Being) is indeed radically unfulfillable in finitude. To quote Sartre again, "The eternity which man is seeking is not the infinity of duration, of that vain pursuit after the self for which I am myself responsible; man seeks a repose in self, the atemporality of the absolute coincidence with himself."[18]

I do not wish here to move forward toward a reflection on the possible goal of that pursuit, the filling of hollowness, the elimination of lack, the dissolution of human loneliness in some fullness of being. I wish to specify further that seeking.

The seeking, as a seeking after meaning, is itself also meaning, where by "meaning" I mean (but the context is the meaning of meaning in Lonergan's *Method in Theology*), in a popular descriptive phrase, "the outgoing of subject"[19]—outgoing from the incarnate human subject of the question of being and of personal identity. Because of the dimensions of that outgoing, all finite response to it is deficient. On the level of a popular consideration of human dialogue one might talk of the asymmetry between speaking and listening. Speaking seems much more abundant than listening. If we were adequately listening to one another's incarnate quested speaking, we would be in a state of habitual genuflection.

At this stage we are slipping from some reflections on the aesthetic context to points whose meaning belong to the religious context, although before touching on the latter we are due to treat of the methodological context. Still, may I remark in a religio-aesthetic interlude that adequate listening and speaking return to the incarnate subject from the environment of men and things insofar as that environment becomes also a meant, a gesture, an outgoing of divine personality. Then the eternity Sartre places as a remote impossibility becomes the facticity of each passing thing. Then the vision which Herman Hesse puts in Goldmund's mouth and mind becomes, not a poet's fancy, but a pilgrim's fact:

> "I believe," he [Goldmund] said to him [Narziss] once, "that the cup of
> a flower, or a little slithering worm on a garden path, says more, and has

more to hide, than all the thousand books in a library. Often, as I write some Greek letter, Theta or Omega, I have only to give my pen a twist, and the letter spreads out, to become a fish, and I, in an instant, am set thinking of all the streams and rivers in the world, of all that is wet and cold; of Homer's sea, and the waters on which Peter walked to Christ. Or else the letter becomes a bird, grows a tail, ruffles out his feathers, and flys off. Well, Narziss, I suppose you think nothing of such letters. But Itell you this: God writes this world with them."[20]

But this facticity rests within a religious horizon, and insofar as that horizon is also Christian the facticity includes a transforming view of personality and conversation, of repentance and regret.

Immediately, however, let us pass to some basic reflections on methodological context. Here I must be brief and indicate partial movements toward that context by reference. The first partial movement is the personal appropriation of such a book as *Insight*, up to p. 388,[21] going beyond that genuinely to the end only insofar as one has taken some authentic stand on the critical realist position on being. The present book is mainly a contribution to this stage.

The second movement is the reorientation of one's science, common sense, and the symbolic and the filling out of a slow-growing-adequate personal *Weltanschauung*.[22] Within that movement is included a precise heuristic conception of man as six- levelled—physical, chemical, botanical, zoological, understanding, religious—or, in more symbolic expression, of individual man as

$$F\ (p_i,\ c_j,\ b_k,\ z_l,\ u_m,\ r_n)^{[23]}$$

and of man in history as

$$H\ S\ddagger\ F\ (p_i,\ c_j,\ b_k,\ z_l,\ u_m,\ r_n).^{[24]}$$

Two further components are required, the first useful, the second essential, to move toward a more axial and personal control of meaning:

(1) The introduction of subscripts and superscripts to indicate stages of meaning and types of meaning.[25]

(2) The fuller implementation of the program of chapter 17 of *Insight*, meshed with that of *Method in Theology*, represented diagrammatically as

$$(\ H\ S\ddagger\ F\ (p_i,\ c_j,\ b_k,\ z_l,\ u_m,\ r_n)\ )\text{--}17\ MIT$$

This implementation requires the communal digestion of man's thinking and feeling about concrete history throughout history and the input of it into the continued emergence of man.[26]

At this point I may remark—without enlarging on it in this present book—that I find the perspective one gradually gets on the globe puts one out of the context of contemporary debates, cold and hot, on capitalism and socialism. As my last endnote in chapter ten indicates, one's view of the GNP and one's feelings about the livability of civilized life become uncomfortably different. Does it lead to utopian dreams? By no means. There is the personal, interpersonal, problem of surviving in all its senses. There is the intimately related problem of appreciating the global relevance of the question posed on a wall in Belfast, "Is there a life before death?" If something is to be done about this *Sickness Unto Death* that palls the end of the second millennium of Christianity, then one must take thought, bring others to take slow radical thought, to relocate the focus of the Wealth of Nations in the Wealth of Selves.

If I am here somewhat autobiographical in my account of the emergence of a methodological context, it seems to me necessary since a methodological context is not a book but the viewpoint of a person. It can develop only slowly, and its emergence is at times more genetical, at times more dialectical, depending on one's teacher, temperament, tribulations, and tradition. It is obviously, however, not a matter of general human authenticity: authenticity demands that one become no more than one is able to become. But it is to be noted that in the measure that the methodological context is neither present to nor suspected by nor respected by those who hold the reins of communal survival and redemption, especially as mediated by the human sciences of psychology, sociology, economics and politics, the survival and redemption will suffer all the horrors of bias. Respected presence of the methodological context belongs to cosmopolis.[27]

One final point regards the relation of the methodological context to loneliness. Riesman's book *The Lonely Crowd* is now history: Loneliness is becoming increasingly a contemporary problem and topic. Still, neither the actuality nor its thematization can blossom in the absence of the methodological context, in which there would be conceived an adequate heuristic of loneliness.[28] One can certainly note descriptively the spectrum of lonelinesses ranging from thin Riesmanian loneliness through various dimensions of loneliness of meaning to mystic loneliness. But that description and those it describes can be implementationally transformed insofar as one conceives heuristically of loneliness in some type of isomorphism with being. So, for example, if man is part "physics" he may have physical achievement and isomorphic dimensions of loneliness. Again, since we are in truth flowers, there is botanical loneliness of various forms. And so on. One can thus parallel the heuristic of being as diagrammed above with an isomorphic diagram of the heuristics of loneliness. One might suspect, too, that a relevant symbolic change of the diagrams above would be the exchange of the two + signs for a $\pm$ sign in each case, thus: $S_{\pm}^{\pm}F$. For, the pure physicochemical level would seem to be only metaphorically lonely (though all creation groans: a consideration of vertical finality would be relevant here), while on the level of divine being there is a negation of loneliness except for the historical bodied-loneliness of the Man-God. So, in these two cases, there is an asymmetry between being and loneliness beyond that which is present in the autonomic forms of finite being.[29]

Such, at any rate, is the indication of the methodological context, and within that personally appropriated context the hermeneutic problem we mentioned earlier takes on in new dimension the reorientation of the common sense, science, and symbolism of thinkers such as Sartre. I mainly touch on Sartre here but obviously there is the lengthier task of reaching out to the various thinkers I mentioned, and beyond them into history, as is indicated in the methodological diagram. Let us then consider a few points, by way of illustration, from Sartre.

First of all I must note that the radical chasm between critical realism and the confused search for a realism in Sartre calls for a methodological recasting of Sartre's basic view, in particular transforming the Nothingness of the for-itself into the loneliness of embodied desire and the tragic anguish of its temporal projects into a theology of finite regret and of healed *ressentiment*. But within that general transformation would be a redemption, for example, of the symbolic dimensions of Sartre's searchings. Again, there are rich considerations within *Being and Nothingness* of Shame and Nausea,[30] the Look,[31] the Body,[32] sexuality, masochism and sadism, coquetry and nakedness,[33] and these considerations, placed in their proper scientific and methodological context, enrich our quest for a redemption of man from "everydayness." So, for example, one might compare Sartre's discussion of Shame to the early discussions of aggression by Konrad Lorenz, in order to appreciate precisely its being only a beginning.[34] So, too, one could compare Sartre's consideration of the mutual incarnate revelation of lovemakers to Lonergan's view on the mediated immediacy of love-making,[35] in order to balance the aberrant realism of Sartre and to redeem the riches of his symbolism and his suggestiveness. And so on.

As you note, I have not treated broader issues here, issues such as the chasm between being and temporality in Heidegger, the relation between being and doing both in Sartre and in de Finance, the split between being and having and the desire that is a growing pain in Marcel,[36] the place of vertical finality in the latter thinking of de Finance. How are these to be transformed into a view of being that is infinite loneliness on the one hand and Infinite Friendship on the other? These are questions for a later day.

Finally, I recall briefly the religious context. I do not personally believe that the other contexts are adequately viable without a religious context and its fruits. Such a context is abundantly indicated by Bernard Lonergan in various parts of *Method in Theology* [37] and in its Catholic strain in his works on the Blessed Trinity and the Incarnation, and from these can be shown to spring a theology of personality, of speaking and of listening, adequately meeting, interiorizing, heightening and transforming the lonelinesses of our present times. But on these I will not expand.[38]

I conclude by recalling now the remarks I made about aesthetic context and the significance of such men as Herman Hesse who was above all a writer of loneliness or homesickness. Our being is a loneliness in search of a mediation of loneliness toward an ultimate transformation of loneliness. Less technically but more tellingly Hesse intimates the same thing toward the end of his novel *Steppenwolf.* The girl Hermine is trying to explain to the forty-year-old Harry Haller why his life is nothing, and yet not nothing:

> "Time and the world, money and power belong to the small people and the shallow people. To the rest, to the real men belongs nothing. Nothing but death."
> "Nothing else?"
> "Yes, eternity."
> "You mean a name, and fame with posterity?"
> "No, Steppenwolf, not fame. Has that any value? And do you think that all true and real men have been famous and known to posterity?"
> "No, of course not."
> "Then it isn't fame. Fame exists in that sense only for the schoolmasters. No, it isn't fame. It is what I call eternity. The pious call it the Kingdom of God. I say to myself: all we who ask too much and have a dimension too many could not contrive to live at all if there were not another air to

breathe outside the air of this world, if there were not eternity at the back of time; and this is the Kingdom of truth. The music of Mozart belongs there and the poetry of your great poets. The saints, too, belong there, who have worked wonders and suffered martyrdom and given a great example to men. But the image of every true act, the strength of every true feeling, belongs to eternity just as much, even though no one knows of it or sees it or records it or hands it down to posterity. . . . Ah, Harry, we have to stumble through so much dirt and humbug before we reach home. And we have no one to guide us. Our only guide is our homesickness.[39]

I may end abruptly. The paradox of my title "Being and Loneliness" is neatly expressed by Heidegger when he writes, "Being is what is nearest [to man]. Yet this near-ness remains farthest removed from him."[40] The existential resolution of this paradox, one might suspect, rests in *Dasein's* acknowledgment, however obscure, of the presence in history of Axial Man who in life was identical on the level of mind, in intentional existence, with total concrete being, and on the level of embodied mind with quintessential loneliness,[41] and who is eternally identical in total embodiment with Prime and Ultimate Being, Infinite Understanding, and Infinite Surprise.

Notes

[1] The epilogue was delivered as a lecture to the *Cogito Society*, University College Cork, under its present title.

[2] Hermann Hesse, *The Journey to the East*, New York, Farrar, Straus & Giroux, 1970, 12.

[3] See B. Lonergan, "The Natural Desire to See God," *Collection*, 84–95; CWL 4, 81–91; at this stage I may recall the footnote on *Insight*, 731 (CWL 3, 754), regarding the adequate context for discussing personal relations. Clearly, modes of personal loneliness require the same context for adequate treatment.

[4] Cited in the beginning of chapter 9 above.

[5] I think of that element in the task of opposing at length Sartre's "Nothingness" with the reality on which it is ultimately based, the root or core of meaning, the *potens omnia* which is the mind of man. Sonic may be puzzled that I made no remark throughout the book on the later Sartre's Marxist Existentialism, so I append two comments. First, in this book I wish to take issue, with Sartre or anyone else, on the presuppositions of any ink-battle prior to taking issue on more complex questions. Secondly, I would echo Raymond Aron's concluding remarks in his discussion of *La Critique de la Raison Dialectique*, "Sartre's Marxism," *Encounter*,

XXIV (1965), no. 6, p. 39: "If Sartre wants to renew Marxist thought in the West, he should model himself on Marx, that is, analyse the capitalist *and* socialist societies of the 20th century. Marxism cannot be renewed by going back from *Das Kapital* to the *Economico-Political Manuscript*, or by trying to achieve some impossible reconciliation between Kierkegaard and Marx.

[6] Quoted by H. G. Gadamer, *Wahrheit and Methode*, 1960, 274, n. 2; also by B. Lonergan, *Method in Theology*, 161; CWL 14, 153.

[7] *Flight to Arras*, London, Heinemann, 1942, 43.

[8] *Tao Te Ching*, Book I, chapter xxvii.

[9] *Method in Theology*, 161; CWL 14, 153.

[10] *Being and Nothingness*, London, Methuen, 1957, 21.

[11] Ibid., 128.

[12] *Being and Having*, London, Fontana, 1965, 181.

[13] From a letter of Edmund Husserl to Franz Brentano, October 15, 1904; quoted in H. Spiegelberg, *The Phenomenological Movement*, Vol. I, The Hague, 1965, 89.

[14] The mention of *Dasein* does not indicate an acceptance of Heidegger's view on embodiment, but I would recall Heidegger's admiration for Rilke's view of the re-collection of man from technicity, and his position on the function of poetry.

[15] I think here of the pursuit outlined in *Insight*. The nature of the pursuit, however, must be determined concretely: see B. Tyrrell, *Lonergan's Philosophy of God*, Gill Macmillan and Notre Dame, 1974.

[16] *Being and Nothingness*, 87–88.

[17] "To a Chinese Girl Singing," *Poems*, Hermann Hesse, Translated by James Wright, London, Cape, 1971, 37.

[18] *Being and Nothingness*, 142.

[19] That "outgoing" at its sublimest can be an identity: *"Eo Magis Unum"*; see B. Lonergan, *Verbum*, 197–201; CWL 2, 204–208.

[20] *Narcissus and Goldmund*, London, Penguin, 1971, 61.

[21] Various people have raised the problem of locating Lonergan's "epistemological question," the second of the three questions mentioned in *Method in Theology* (pp. 25, 83, 261, 316; CWL 14, pp. 27, 80, 245, 294). To my mind the epistemological question is answered by the "breakthrough, envelopment and confinement" described on p. 484 (CWL 3, 508) of *Insight*, and indicated between pp. 319 and 388 (CWL 3, 343–413).

[22] I have left inkmarks of my own efforts in the two books *Randomness, Statistics, and Emergence*, Gill Macmillan and Notre Dame, 1970 [2nd edition, Vancouver, Axial Publishing, 2021], dealing mainly with the methodology of the natural sciences, and *Plants and Pianos*, Milltown Institute, Dublin, 1971 [*The Shaping of the Foundations*,

University Press of America, 1976, pp. 1–73], dealing with contemporary issues in the methodology of botany and music.

23 The letters in the function stand for the levels of conjugates, b = botanical, u = understanding, etc. The subscripts indicate the range of conjugates on that level, e.g., p_6 might refer to a gravitational conjugate systematically formulated in a space-time geometry (See *Randomness, Statistics, and Emergence*, pp. 114–120; 2nd edition pp. 95–100). The placing of the religious as a sixth level will undoubtedly puzzle some readers. It is part of my own heuristics in the context of my faith (for a symbolic expression of the latter, see my *Music That Is Soundless*, Milltown Institute, Dublin, 1969). Others may be content with **a** five-levelled heuristic of material reality. How are the levels related? To grasp that adequately is a tricky personal enterprise: See *Randomness, Statistics, and Emergence*, especially chapter 9; also *Insight*, on randomness, genera, species.

24 The entire expression is obviously only an aid to heuristic conception. Some of the symbols need little further explanation. H = History, as heuristically conceived through *Method in Theology* in the context of emergent probability (on the latter, see *Randomness, Statistics, and Emergence* chapter 11). S = the sum of contemporaneous men, a loose heuristic. The upper + adds the heuristic of chapter 19 of *Insight*. The lower + adds the non-human environment. Symbolic images like these, or my earlier diagrams, or the "display" of the good in *Method in Theology* (p. 48; CWL 14, 47), may or may not be helpful to the individual, but some images are necessary: A discussion of this underpinning of intentional existence would be a lengthy aside. As an exercise in heuristics and in heuristic diagramming one might ask the metaeconomic question, "Where would one locate Fortune's 500 or The Times' 1000?"

25 Cf. "Zoology and the Future of Philosophers" footnote 42 (see footnote 4 of chapter 1). There I discuss **a** way **of** indicating various meanings of, e.g., aggression. For example, a_{1i} corresponds to some commonsense grasp, a_{2j} to some theoretic grasp, a_{3m}, to some grasp within the nod of interiority. Again, a^{bcp} could indicate the level of explanation reached, b, c, and p each taking on possibilities 1 to 3, e.g., a^{211} would indicate what is described as "the second step" in *Insight*, p. 464 (CWL 3, 489), where biophysics and biochemistry have not yet entered in; a^{333} would indicate an adequate heuristic of animal aggression-which of course presupposes some familiarity with lower superscript values. Again, one's heuristic can be helped by a consideration of the possible sub-functions of any of the level variables, and of the space-time conditionedness of the functions. Such a procedure may help one to openness in the *a posteriori* questioning, e.g., of the variation from life to non-life of the virus (see *Plants and Pianos*, 41), or of considerations of the separated soul (*Summa Theologica*, Ia, q. 89). Of course, one does not need such advanced heuristics

to raise the existential question which must at some time spring from the notion of survival: "What is it to die?"

[26] See *Insight*, 543, 740–43; CWL 3, 566–67, 761–64. In chapter 10 I noted the relation of part 3 of Lowe's *On Economic Knowledge* to the feedback procedure.

[27] See *Insight*, chapter 7. By cosmopolis is not meant, of course, the concrete institutions of the Christian churches: they, too, are in need of a physician. I mean, rather, radical concrete fidelity to the intention of being, the notion of survival. That concrete fidelity is itself conditioned in the manner described by B. Tyrrell, *op. cit.*, endnote 15 above.

[28] Thomists will question here my use of loneliness as an apparently basic category. Am I stretching Aquinas's *dolor*, *tristitia*, etc., metaphorically beyond all bounds? A consideration of this would, I think, entail an elaboration of the relation of the present effort with that of *Etre et Agir*, a consideration of the nature, increase and decrease of habits, and a reflection on the psychology of language. See also endnote 38.

[29] Autonomic and synnomic forms are defined in *Plants and Pianos*, p. 40.

[30] These two, *Being and Nothingness*, *passim* part 4.

[31] Ibid., 252–302.

[32] Ibid., 303–535.

[33] These five, *passim* 361–412.

[34] Cf. P. McShane, "Zoology and the Future of Philosophers" (see endnote 4 of chapter 1).

[35] *Method in Theology*, 77; CWL 14, 75.

[36] *Being and Having*, 146–47, 164–89.

[37] Cf. the index under *Gift*.

[38] The problem is closely related to the development of a new spirituality, meshing such streams as the Franciscan, the Carmelite, the Ignatian and negative mysticisms of East and West into a new objective interiority.

[39] Hermann Hesse, London, Penguin, 1971, 178–79.

[40] "Letter on Humanism." Cf. W. Richardson, *Heidegger: Through Phenomenology to Thought*, 10.

[41] For a discussion of the ground of that loneliness see F. E. Crowe, S.J., "Eschaton in the Mind and Heart of Jesus," *The Eschaton: A Community of Love*, Villanova University Press, 1974; *Appropriating the Lonergan Idea*, ed. Michael Vertin, Washington, The Catholic University of America Press, 1989, pp. 193–234.

Postlude: Prelude to
Process: A Paideiad[1]

In the corner of a Dublin pub
This party opens—blub-a-blub—
Paddy Whiskey, Rum and Gin
Paddy Three sheets in the wind;
Paddy of the Celtic Mist,
Paddy Connemara West,
Chestertonian Paddy Frog
Croaking nightly in the bog.
All the Paddies having fun
Since Yeats handed in his gun.
Every man completely blind
To the truth about his mind.[2]

Aeacus: Poetry is to be weighed in the scales.
Xanthias: What? How can tragedy be weighed?
Aeacus: They will bring rulers and compasses to measure the words, and
those forms which are used for molding bricks. . . .[3]

Maybe there is still a moment to interrupt that process of willed deafness
which is nearly total already. It lies, of course, with the defenders of
objectivity to rescue it from that sterility in which it labours at the moment,
in the last agony of a concern for method. . . .[4]

Notes

[1] The title of a work in process to emerge in the 1980s, with chapter headings: 1.
"Procedural Analytiks," 2. "Instrumental Acts of Meaning," 3. "General Heuristiks,"
4. "Intentional Process," 5. "Eternal Process," 6. "Total Process," Paideiad is related
to the meaning of Paideia in both Greek and Hebrew traditions; not unrelated to
Kavanagh's "Paddiad" (See following endnote).

[2] Patrick Kavanagh, "The Paddiad," *Collected Poems*, Martin Brian and O'Keeffe Ltd,
London, 1964, 90.

[3] Aristophanes, *The Frogs.*

[4] Roger Poole, *Towards Deep Subjectivity*, Harper Torchbooks, New York, 1972, 43.

Index

ABOUT THE AUTHOR

Philip McShane (February 18, 1932–July 1, 2020) was an Irish Canadian mathematician, philosopher, economist, and theologian. He earned an M.Sc. in relativity theory and quantum mechanics with First Honors from University College, Dublin (1952–56), where he lectured in mathematics before doing his D.Phil. at Oxford (1965–68)

Once describing himself as "a dabbler, a mathematician gone astray, rambling in the worlds of economics and literature, music and physics," McShane published works ranging from the foundations of mathematics, probability theory, and evolutionary process to essays on the philosophy of education and interpretation. He also wrote introductory texts focusing on critical thinking, linguistics, and economics.

Many consider McShane the leading interpreter of Bernard Lonergan's (1904–1984) *Insight: A Study of Human Understanding*, a compendious work that lays out both a genetic method for studying organic development and canons for a methodological hermeneutics. For over fifty years McShane was profoundly influenced by Lonergan's major works in economics and his breakthrough discovery of the dynamics of global collaboration

In the last years of his life, McShane wrote with increasing clarity about the negative Anthropocene age in which we live and a future positive Anthropocene age of methodological luminosity and glocal collaboration. In *Economics for Everyone* (2017, 3rd edition), he indicated crucial steps for seeding the positive age when the "cultural overhead" of leisure will be understood, taught, and practiced, thus freeing many and all increasingly to pursue activities leading to genuine human development.

When McShane died in the summer of 2020, friends, colleagues, and former students around the globe paid tribute to him. One person described him as an "African elder," another as someone who "gave counsel to think long-term, in terms of centuries rather than years or even decades," and a third as "someone I could always be myself around, even when I was angsty, anxious, or depressed … a friend, mentor, professor, and family member all at once." A former student described "being amazed, when I asked him some questions, at his generosity — he tore out a chapter of something he was working on and gave it to me there and then."

OTHER BOOKS BY THE AUTHOR

Randomness, Statistics, and Emergence, 2nd ed. (2021)
Interpretation from A to Z (2020)
The Future: Core Precepts in Supramolecular Method and Nanochemistry (2019)
Economics for Everyone: Das Jus Kapital, 3rd ed. (2017)
The Allure of the Compelling Genius of History (2015)
Piketty's Plight and the Global Future (2014)
The Everlasting Joy of Being Human (2013)
The Road to Religious Reality: Method in Theology 101 AD 9011 (2012)
Bernard Lonergan: His Life and Leading Ideas (with Pierrot Lambert) (second printing 2013)
Lack in the Beingstalk: A Giants Causeway (2007)
Introducing Critical Thinking (with Alexandra Drage and John Benton) (2005)
Pastkeynes Pastmodern Economics: A Fresh Pragmatism (2000)
A Brief History of Tongue (1998)
Lonergan's Challenge to the University and the Economy (1980)
The Shaping of the Foundations (1976)
Wealth of Self and Wealth of Nations (1973)
Music That Is Soundless (1968)

WORKS EDITED BY THE AUTHOR

Do You Want a Sane Global Economy? (2010)
For a New Political Economy (Collected Works of Bernard Lonergan, volume 21, 1999)
Phenomenology and Logic: The Boston College Lectures on Mathematical Logic and Existentialism (Collected Works of Bernard Lonergan, volume 18, 2001)
Searching for Cultural Foundations (1984)
Language, Truth, and Meaning (1972)

WEBSITE ESSAY SERIES
(http://www.philipmcshane.org/essay-series)

Questing 2020	*Posthumous*
LO and Behold	*Bridgepoise*
Æcornomics	*Eldorede*
Interpretation	*Field Nocturnes*
Disputing Quests	*Cantowers*

www.ingramcontent.com/pod-product-compliance
Lightning Source LLC
LaVergne TN
LVHW051646080426
835511LV00016B/2527